TECHNIQUES
FOR
THE
SERIOUS
INVESTOR

Real Estate Concepts, Strategies, Investment Plans, and Perspec̄es

by
H. Roger Neal

Myriad Publishing, Incorporated
Dublin, Ohio

Printed in the United States of America
First Edition, First Printing

Cover design: Joelle Dulaney
Cover illustration: Joelle Dulaney
Cover colors: Nancy Neal

Library of Congress Catalog Card Number: 95-080307

ISBN 0-9648580-1-0

Myriad Publishing, Inc.
P.O. Box 1109
Dublin, Ohio 43017-1109
(614) 792-1579

Acknowledgments

My special thanks to Nancy Neal, Roger Neal, Tami Chilcutt, and Paul Norris for their technical support. To Vera Thornhill for her desktop publishing skills and to Randy Edwards for his mathematical proofreading. To Attorney John Neal for his contract assistance. And a special thanks to Joelle Dulaney for a superb and motivating cover design.

All real estate investing involves some level of risk. What Neal purports to explain is what he has accomplished and deduced. He is not an attorney, nor an accountant. He does council with them often, as he advises for you to do so as well. He is just a successful investor.

It is important to know the laws for your region regarding contracts, business practices, and procedures. Furthermore, it is important to keep abreast of the ever changing tax laws as well. Simply take the ideas and adapt them to your respective region and the times.

Dedication

To my sweet child, Katelyn, whose
miraculous recovery from her automobile
accident exhibited her inner strength and
veracity to overcome enormous obstacles.
Her spunk, enthusiasm, and ambition should
be a lesson to us all.

Table of Contents

Introduction

Most readers of my first book, *Streetwise Investing In Rental Housing*, find me a very conservative real estate investor who keeps nearly everything he buys. This observation is half right, I am very conservative with my investments, and this book will take no exception. But I do have other strategies and perspectives, which they may be unaware, where I do sell properties. These strategies and perspectives include collecting a vast income from notes which I literally created for myself. These other techniques include the opportunity of making money on properties that I never buy and magnifying wealth by using the right tax shelters.

Furthermore, I am primarily notable for that book in composing a self generating career in real estate for those with dead end jobs, like I had, for others locked in $60,000 per year jobs who want their lives back, and for those who want to passively make more money by employing relatives. That assessment is totally accurate.

Who would guess that I also receive a hefty source of monthly income from notes through the resale of properties? Just because I have maintained a portfolio of investment properties, and am quite successful at it, I could be perceived as one dimensional, a landlord.

Conversely, there are many other aspects to my overall program which led to my success.

Introduction

Introduction

In fact, because of other creative ideas, I have sheltered income that under ordinary circumstances would have been swallowed up by federal taxes. That sheltered income was reinvested and parlayed, so to speak. Furthermore, not only did this same shelter virtually permit me to double my investment capital, but still granted me the opportunity to make a tidy sum on cash flow. This medium is the **Low Income Housing Tax Credit** program. Compile this with **Installment Sales Income** and **1031 Tax Free Exchanges** and watch the tax problems dissipate.

In addition, over the years I have developed ways to further my profit, and not only by the proverbial cost cutting methods. Most seasoned investors just about have that mastered. Rather, by orchestrating closings with notes and mortgages prepared strategically in my favor, I have been able to multiply profit beyond belief.

You will also find 5 Investment Plans outlined to choose from based upon your own individual investment needs, financial abilities, aspirations, and, of course, tolerance. These are founded from my own experiences in **note creation**. My aim was to produce additional monthly income without additional responsibilities. Selling off unwanted properties was just an added bonus for me.

Depending upon your current job status, financial needs, ability, and the time you devote to real estate, your creation of notes, and their applications will vary. For these reasons I have created and outlined these plans whereby investors are free to decide for themselves to implement any combination of 1, 2, 3, 4, or all 5 plans singly, or simultaneously.

None of the plans are get-rich-quick schemes, rather they are systematic and methodical techniques to increase wealth and income over a long period of time, not in just 90 days or 1 year. (Sorry, you won't be rich by Christmas!)

Below is an overview of all five plans. In the upcoming chapters, each plan has a fully detailed layout, with very conservative learning examples.

If you find that Plans I, IV, and V are the only plans that you are capable of implementing due to your own financial restrictions, please read through Plans II and III anyway because you could find some ideas that could apply to your current situation, or even enable you to modify Plans I, IV, or V.

Although I have five moneymaking programs that go from start to finish, both keepers and sellers of portfolios can learn from the techniques to correctly situate their portfolios or just sell them. Investors can feel free to extract ideas from their context, whenever feasible. On the other hand, if you want full detailed plans, just select the ones right for you.

Synopsis Of Note Creation Plans.

Investment Plan I.

Plan I offers seasoned landlords refuge from tenants by offering a **FAST-FLIP** program, eliminating long term tenant relationships and repairs.

Less than $4,000 cash is needed to start and fully implement this plan, one project at a time. Of course, simultaneous projects require more investment capital. This plan can be adopted by investors with either small or large sums of capital. Those with small amounts of investment capital can withdraw their input at resale. Others can opt to sell with little to nothing down in order to obtain even larger notes.

Plan I can also be used as a SLOW-FLIP program by simply stalling the process. However, no examples have been provided.

Investment Plan II.

Plan II recommends and poses abstract thinking and complex applications for the expert investors who desire new strategies for improving their profit pictures. Also, it is a vehicle to transform unprofitable rentals to profitable notes.

After you have established some base of income, whether it is from real estate, another career, spouse, and have your living expenses met with money to spare you can implement this technique. Landlords who can afford to sell now with virtually no immediate return can expect to magnify their returns later by waiting just a few short years.

This plan is not a FAST-FLIP program as in Plan I, rather a **FAST-SELL** program. This program is to be implemented with properties with high equity and whose majority of loan payments goes toward the principle rather than the interest. Examples 5A and 5B have both been originated with short term assumable financing and were in their final years of payoff.

Plan II does not necessarily mean that you have more than $4,000 invested. Although your finances may be limited, you may decide to execute Plan II on a property you have owned for some time. I am simply recommending that you increase your monthly income first through immediate income producing notes so that delayed income notes you acquire are not jeopardized by everyday living expenses. Without the proper income base, negative cash flows can be dangerous.

This technique also appeals to those like me who maintain a steady pool of tenants and lavish in collecting rents and tax write-offs.

After reading the specifics of Plan II in its entirety, you may even decide to restructure future purchases on properties that you plan to keep in your portfolio in order to conform to this brilliant selling method in the future.

Furthermore, you will discover a new way to unload a loser and ultimately profit enormously by doing so. Example 5B illustrates just how to do so.

Investment Plan III.

Unequivocally, this Plan is for investors who want to sell at least one loan-free property and also provides an outlet for investors with cash sums, of $20,000 and up, who desire a program for investing their own money to **FAST-FLIP**. In essence, equity or cash amounts will be exchanged for much larger notes, payable monthly and immediately.

Depending upon the length of time the properties are held, tax benefits and cash flow may or may not be of consequence. If Plan III is utilized in a FAST-FLIP program, they are not to be considered an important factor in your final profit schedule. On the other hand, if you choose to hold properties at length in a **SLOW-FLIP**, then they both do add a flavor to the overall profit picture.

Plan III also offers an alternative to cashing out when there are no buyers for your properties: be they overpriced, lacking good repair, or too lowly purchased for minimum bank loans. Installment sales, as opposed to cash, also add a flair to income and plays an integral role in tax considerations.

Investment Plan IV.

This plan is the lowest cost to implement and provides a detailed layout on exactly how to **FAST-FLIP** residential and small commercial properties with an **Option To Purchase** without ever buying a single property. The beauty of this technique is that you will never take title to any deeds, yet you will profit just like owners who sell their properties. You will never be a landlord or an owner. Amazingly, you will profit from the equity just the same.

Plan IV is the solution to all obstacles and objections such as no investment cash, risk and liability, no time for real estate ownership, repairs, tenants, and overall bad experiences with real estate investing in the past. You will find the OPTION TO PURCHASE surprising, exciting, and quite profitable.

Investors with large established portfolios can further their expertise on property acquisition and disposition. They can heavily utilize Plans I, II, III, and V on existing properties and dabble with Plan IV.

Investment Plan V.

Here is the opportunity to **FAST-FLIP** and still maintain control of the property. Single homes are ideal for this plan because you seek want-to-be homeowners. It is a very conservative approach which integrates a 3 year trial run through a **Lease With The Option To Purchase**, and finally culminates with a Land Sales Contract. The solution to the owner occupied down payment problem is solved in this plan.

You've often heard about investors who have resold the same property over and over again who have heavily profited by doing so. Upon a buyer's default within the first 3 years, you keep the option fee, monthly rent, and all monthly option payments. Here is your opportunity to benefit from a buyer performing or defaulting.

This plan will also accommodate a **SLOW-FLIP** course of action. In fact, you can acquire singles on 8 year payouts. After payoff, begin the Lease-Option program.

I have witnessed some very risky, and successful, investment techniques, five of which I will explain, critique, and rate with a thumb's up or thumb's down. Although they are not of my creation, I do recommend some twists. They are also some of the newest, innovative ideas, and popular methods currently being used nationally.

After achieving success with income and net worth, be it through *Steetwise* applications or otherwise, your mind returns to earlier dreams and ambitions because now you can fulfill them. There is nothing wrong with that either. My dream from the start has always been to own a large apartment complex in an upscale end of town, and it still is. It remains unfulfilled today because the income from my inner city rentals is so far superior than that of the nicer type rentals, making the transition difficult to digest. That option, though, remains open to me now, whereas when I began in real estate, it did not.

If you have read my first book and succeeded much in the same way, you can choose to continue onward and add to your income with the knowledge of this second book.

Conversely, now may be the time to sell out your existing portfolio, dabble with note creation for easy income, and go buy that restaurant, golf course, or whatever that has always been your dream. This book will aid you in the selling off of your portfolio, and provide you with additional income and assets, if you so desire.

Even those knowledgeable investors who have been out of the business for awhile will predictably find the information refreshing, innovative, deep, and sometimes profound. Hopefully, it will rekindle their investment fever.

These concepts and techniques will even provide some investors the dream of a lifetime. They can get close to real estate without getting any of it on them.

After investing and interacting with other investors since 1979 and society at large, I have concluded that the biggest obstacle to achieving financial independence is the investor himself. For that reason, I have detailed my own core philosophy, herein being the solution to failure.

Read, study, learn, and implement. Your future awaits you!

PART 1
5 PLANS TO
NOTE CREATION

CHAPTER 1

CREATING NOTES: FUNDAMENTAL APPLICATIONS

Investor Profile.

These techniques of buying for immediate resale, flipping, to create mortgage notes are designed for and appeals from dabblers who wish to maintain other careers to those who invest on a full time basis in real estate. It enables both types of investors to create an additional source, and type, of income much different than the traditional monthly cash flow and capital gains from resale. However, these methods are not recommended as a sole endeavor unless and until an acceptable level of income and wealth accumulation has been achieved.

If you are an investor who desires only to invest part-time, you will find that illusive position you seek which enables you to own real estate without the entangled landlord-tenant relationships.

With the **Fast-Flip** in Plans I and IV, you can avoid most of the pitfalls associated with tenants and repairs. Tenants are constantly on the move. Each time a vacancy occurs, the landlord must return to the premises and bring everything back to acceptable city code conditions. Depending upon the tenant, this continuous tenant damage could be both time consuming and expensive. For me, it is a hassle

INVESTOR TOLERANCE

-PLANS-

Ideal for investors who:	I	II	III	IV	V
have no money.				●	
have at least $4,000 to invest.	●	●		●	●
have $20,000 and up to invest.	●	●	●	●	●
can tolerate tenants.	●	●	●	●	●
absolutely hates tenants.				●	
can make, or direct, a few repairs.	●	●	●	●	●
refuse to make any repairs.				●	
do not own any property now.	●	●	●	●	●
want to just dabble in real estate	●		●	●	●
are full-time now in real estate and want additional income.	●	●	●	●	●
own dozens of properties.	●	●	●	●	●
want to sell off existing properties.	●	●	●		●
desire conservative risk taking only.	●	●	●	●	●
can't handle any risk.				●	
are novices.					
are seasoned or experts.	●	●	●	●	●

more than it is expensive. Furthermore, I find that most of my inner-city tenants move quite often. If the flip from buying to selling is swift enough, you can avoid the brunt of these drawbacks. The FAST-FLIP is ideal for investors who desire to avoid tenants, yet still yearn to invest in real estate.

On the other hand, if you are an investor, like myself, who invests exclusively in real estate as a career and keeps a steady pool of tenants, you too will enjoy this diversion and challenge in accumulating cash from balloon payments and additional income from long-term monthly payments. Naturally, you will maintain a portfolio of rentals for a steady income to sustain a good lifestyle, but this particular method of creating notes offers an added source of cash and income which you can pile onto your current monthly cash flow and existing cash reserves.

Target Buyers.

The majority of buyers you will target for the first four plans are investors. Investors are more preferable to buy your properties because of their greater financial ability to repay. That is why you will primarily focus the FAST-FLIP on small multi-families. Within this price and down payment range, the majority of activity will be from 2-4 units. So, except for Plan V, owner-occupants will probably not be interested in this property type. Larger apartment buildings that are feasible for these plans will be lower in number. Not only will they require larger down payments, which exceeds their boundaries, but there will be fewer sellers willing to carry financing.

Investors do buy single homes, as I do. However, my purpose for that type of investment is much different for Plan V. The problem here is that by the time you slap a second mortgage on them, there is not much cash flow due to their only being one rent, which is unattractive to most. It is possible to integrate singles into Plan I, but more likely into Plans II, III, IV, and V. Insofar as the first four plans are concerned, I recommend your primary focus to be on small multi-families to attract a larger pool of investors and quicker sales.

Plan V, though, is specifically designed to attract homeowners. It is a very unorthodox plan, which is detailed in Chapter 8. If your forte is singles, you will find a new approach easy to integrate into your current strategy.

On the whole, investors can more easily come up with the larger down payments that you will require, can buy and own more than one property at a time, and are more capable of making balloon payments. Furthermore, the depth of financial resources of investors far exceeds that of homeowners in the low-income neighborhoods. For example, an investor who earns $65,000 per year on his job will buy your property for investment purposes, but he will not live there. A person earning $15,000 per year will live there and will scrounge to come up with the measly 3% FHA minimum down payment.

In fact, the down payment you require from your buyer will far exceed the 3% and 5% FHA homeowner requirements. For example, FHA only requires 3% down payment on the first $25,000 and 5% above $25,000. If the purchase price is under $50,000, the entire down payment remains at the 3%. This is absolutely fantastic for sellers of single homes to homeowners.

Consider selling a property for $35,000. The 3% FHA requirement can be met with only $1,050. This is how this class of buyers acquire homes in these neighborhoods.

So if bank financing is so great, why don't you buy and sell single homes to owner-occupants that way? Many other good investment plans call for doing so, but this is not the strategy or market for any of my plans. Your strategy is to acquire properties that are the easiest for you to purchase and fastest to unload. Turn-around-time for your buyer to qualify for his loan, passing inspections, and dealing with selling commissions are just too many obstacles and expenses to overcome with a limited investment, $4,000 per project. The traditional loan process is also too slow and involved for such a small project return featured in most of my conservative plans anyway.

In fact, it is illegal for banks not to make loans to qualified buyers in these undesirable areas. It is called redlining. Strategically, banks have simply increased the amount of their minimum mortgage loan. If the smallest loan is $40,000, for example, it would be difficult for a buyer to finance a property costing $35,000. It has, indeed, made it a hardship for both buyers and sellers.

More importantly for my programs, the homeowner-type buyers in these neighborhoods are less capable of performing on $4,000 down payments and on 1 to 3 year balloons than investors. You want to **get in and get out** as fast as you can, and get your cash investment back at closing.

Granted, this is not true in all cases. It is, however, remotely possible to sell to an owner-occupant, in these particular neighborhoods, who even pays cash for the entire purchase price for either a single, double, row, or apartment building. Of course, if they qualify for your terms, you will sell to them.

My programs really cater, though, to the most probable sellers, buyers, contracts, and profit outcomes. With this logic, I will deliberately overlook less likely scenarios.

Financing For You And Your Buyers.

This strategy requires your seller to carry the financing or your seller's mortgage company to continue the existing financing. Since you are creating the financing arena for your buyers, they will not initially need to obtain bank financing. In fact, if your note does not call for a balloon payment, your buyer will not be required to refinance unless he resells and you have installed a due-on-sale clause. Buyers find this most appealing.

In order to appropriately set the stage for a quick turnover with an easy assumption upon resale, you too must stay away from banks. You can't hardly obtain non-assumable loans and expect to provide financing for your buyers. If you do sell on Land Sales Contract under these conditions, you are creating an atmosphere of foreclosure. Find existing loans that are assumable for your buyers.

If necessary, borrow the $4,000, even $8,000 or $12,000, for start-up costs on as many projects as you can handle. Remember, these amounts are to be retrieved in the short run. Just insure that the funds are not legally attached to properties that you want to flip. Use a credit card or home equity loan, if necessary. You want to withdraw, invest, and repay funds at will. I would reserve this technique for those with surety.

The environment which you will create for yourself is one where everything is legal and above board. To accomplish this framework, you must confine yourself to FHA, VA, Purchase Money Mortgage assumable loans, and cash deals, i.e., if cash is abound.

Just because you assume a loan does not necessarily mean that the loan is again assumable by your buyer. Some assumable loans are conventional loans. They are only assumable one time with a complete credit application and loan approval. It can also be assumable if a bank fears default coming and you are their escape plan. Often, this assumable loan requires a fee of $150-250 and 4 to 6 weeks to close. It's not that bad except that usually no one can assume the loan from you. This is a problem at resale.

FHA and VA loans are quick and low cost assumable loans that are very desirable to you. The buyer needs only $125 to assume the loan. However, FHA loans originated after 12-1-86 require that the they be held by the original mortgagee for at least 2 years before they are assumable. Concentrate on FHA loans originated before 12-1-86 and ones held over or near two years obtained afterward. If the loan is only 21 months old, you can easily delay the closing for 3 months. If the loan is assumed after 2 years and that buyer wishes to sell, he need not hold the unit for an additional 2 years. This applies only to the original mortgagee.

Even more recent stipulations are the FHA as of 12-14-89 require and the VA as of 3-1-88 that buyers qualify by the lenders before assumptions are made. This is not really an obstacle because most loans that I encounter are around ten years old and have the necessary equity to enable the plans to work.

Interest rates on FHA and VA loans are not as an important factor as you might think. If current rates are 9 percent and the existing loan is 13 percent, this does not necessarily mean that you will rule out this property. The purchase price, balance of loan, and the payment will altogether determine your decision. In fact, I've even assumed loans at 17 percent.

There are lending institutions who **streamline** balances on FHA and VA loans, whereby the current mortgagee owns the property for at least 6 months, has paid on the loan in a timely fashion, and has a responsible credit history. This is a good selling point upon resale. Advise your buyer to pay on a timely basis and maintain a good credit rating. After the 6 month waiting period, your buyer can try to streamline the interest rate with little or no money down in most cases. Closing costs can often be built into the loan. Lenders have advised me that at least a 2 percent or more reduction in current percentage points makes streamlining worthwhile, taking into consideration the balance of the loan term. As a general rule, more than two percentage points makes it feasible.

On one of my portfolio properties, I streamlined with a company who specializes in existing FHA loans, where equity withdrawal was forbidden, and the loans are again assumable after a 2-year waiting period. Not only did my PITI payment drop from $315 to $286, but the length of the loan was reduced from 24 to 20 years.

Don't confuse this with the usual refinancing method. Streamlining is only offered by few companies and it is a feature offered only to those holding FHA and VA loans.

Streamlining is for your buyers, not for you or your seller. Holding properties for six months is not within the parameters of the FAST-FLIP.

Before you advertise an assumable loan for sale with a high interest rate you will research for a mortgage lender who provides this streamline service and provide that company name and phone number to your prospective buyer during your negotiations. Be sure to state that he must meet their qualifications and is welcome to call them immediately to check your information. Advise only that he should verify your information and get further details himself. Inform him that you cannot accurately gauge his credit worthiness because you are neither a loan officer nor an underwriter. You are simply expressing a possible avenue or idea for your buyer to consider.

Purchase Money Mortgages are the third and final mortgages to assume, and in some cases create, in order to provide financing for your buyers. A Purchase Money Mortgage is a loan provided solely by and directly from the seller. When originating a PMM when you are the buyer, specify that the loan is assumable. Conversely, when selling, specify that the loan is not assumable without your written permission. (Likewise, Land Sales Contracts should have such a clause.)

The property must have no loan balance to originate and is possible to assume. The deed is transferred to the buyer at closing, just like the FHA and VA assumptions, and is secured with a mortgage and note payable to the seller, as if he were the bank.

FHA, VA, and PMM's are the only existing mortgages from which you are to choose. PMM's are the only loans you create. This limits the availability of purchases, and your down payment even further restricts your market with these plans. If you wish to avoid the pitfalls associated with seller financing (unauthorized Land Sales Contracts and forbidden loan assumptions), and desire to buy and sell in an ultra conservative manner, this is absolutely the only way to safely implement the plan.

Don't Buy, But Sell-On Land Sales Contract!

Do not buy or assume existing Land Sales Contracts because of the enormous drawbacks associated with not getting the deeds. However, you can sell on Land Sales Contract to your buyers, laws permitting.

NEVER BUY ON LAND SALES CONTRACT, SELL ON LAND SALES CONTRACT.

The reason for this extreme guideline, and many others forthcoming, on the assumability aspect is to prepare the properties for quick resale. Speed is a primary consideration. Even priced right, I've seen properties set for six months and much longer.

I had a neighbor who tried to sell his house for four years with conventional financing, two of which while he was living in another state. If he had an assumable loan with a low down payment, I am sure that the property would have sold immediately.

In essence, assumable loans with no release of liability, with low down payments, as compared to all other financing, are the easiest and fastest properties to buy and resell. This is the fundamental concept to the successful implementation of these plans.

This technique does not include pro- visions for leaving the closing table with thousands of dollars by bleeding properties of all their equity. However, leaving the buying table with $500 does not jeopardize the property, risk factor, nor your profit.

Get Small Down Payments From Buyers.

Although you will be assuming and creating loans without financial institutions, there is still a need for down payments and repair money. Receiving a $500 credit at closing to a $2,000 down payment for yourself is most desirable. Couple this with an additional $2,000 in repair money and your first project will cost a maximum of $4,000 after selling expenses. You will require the cash that you invested, up to $4,000, from your buyer at closing. The goal is to get your money right back out of the property.

Insofar as your buyer is concerned, down payments under $4,000 is very appealing. A down payment of $2,000 will further hasten the sale.

Cash Investors.

On the other hand, if you choose to modify the plans by investing with all cash, your investment will far exceed the $4,000. In fact, your buyer's down payment can even be zero. Your compensation can be even a higher price than one with a down payment of $4,000, and a higher interest rate. Familiarize yourself with your state's legal maximum interest rate which you can charge on first, second, and third mortgages.

Balloon Payments.

When cash is needed for multiple projects, personal reasons, balloons, or to eliminate the need for partners could solve those problems. Balloon payments are where the entire balance of the loan is due on a specified date. I've found that most balloons come due in 1 to 3 years. All the figures and terms remain as agreed, except a balloon date is included.

You can clump all the mortgages on a property together in a balloon with a Land Sales Contract or wrap, or just in a balloon note payable to you, a 2nd mortgage for example.

It is wisest to balloon just the mortgage payable to you. For example, it would be easier for the buyer to come up with your $10,000 note than $25,500 including the first mortgage. The buyer in this situation has the option to either pay just you or refinance the entire balance and pay off both mortgages. Providing a choice gives the buyer more flexibility and makes the deal more attractive.

Balloons are also a good outlet to utilize to compensate for mistakes that you have made. For example, if you have underestimated the repair costs by $1,000 you can institute the same $10,000 note coupled with an additional and separate $1,000 note payable in two 3-month $500 installments. Providing the buyer is receptive to balloons, you can even balloon your entire note balance of $11,000 in two years if cash is really needed. Whatever the case, this plan demands you to regain your cash investment in the shortest period of time. Simply, when you are short on cash, ask for balloon payments.

On the other hand, if you have large cash reserves, it will not be necessary to squeeze your buyer out of another $1,000 in cash. You can simply create a note for $11,000 rather than $10,000. Ultimately, the trade-off will be to invest $1,000 and receive a note for $11,000. It is not as good as getting all of your money back and having a note for $10,000, but it is still a successful endeavor.

Balloon payments are in the same arena as Land Sales Contracts. Never buy or assume notes with balloon payments, but you can sell with them. These procedures are to keep the investments conservative and reduce pitfalls. Balloons can blow up!

- **NEVER BUY BALLOONS,**
- **SELL WITH BALLOONS.**

I don't like to pressure buyers, not meaning pressure to initiate a balloon, rather the pressure incurred at the time the balloon is due. I don't want the properties back. I prefer long term notes anyway. To me, CASH is a four letter word. I prefer income.

From the time I received my first note many years ago, I have acquired many others encompassing both short and long terms, some with balloons, hence Plans I-V. Overall, my preference leans towards the more lengthy of notes with only a few balloons. However, I do admit that balloons are difficult to resist. Maintaining a variety of 10, 15, 20, and 30 year notes with intermittent balloons is the best income strategy when you are building wealth. Afterward, when tax considerations enter the forefront, don't sell with balloon payments. (This will be discussed further in Chapters 9 and 12.)

There is also a strategy, of course, which includes inserting balloons on every deal and not worrying whether the balloon clauses are fulfilled or not. The whole idea is to renegotiate price, terms, monthly payment, interest rate, and/or more cash down at the time of default. If it weren't for buyer's performing, it wouldn't be such a bad idea. However, in my case, the tax ramifications are a deterrent, as will be discussed in Chapter 9.

Price Range.

Since these plans are conservative, you will invest in the low-income segment of investment property in an older, dilapidated section of the inner city. If you are on the hook for a total of $20,000-30,000, how much can you possibly lose? Comparatively speaking, if you invest $60,000 in a property, what is the absolute maximum you can lose? Obviously, you will not lose your entire investment on either deal. I only posed those rhetorical questions to merely illustrate that if losses were to transpire, there is more to lose as the investment dollars increase. As you minimize your investment, so minimizes your risk. In this price range, so increases the profit potential as well.

Although that is an excellent reason to invest in low end properties, it is secondary only to the wider availability of prospective investment opportunities from which to profit. In other words, there are more properties for you to choose from with $1,000 down in the $20,000 range than in the $60,000 range, or $160,000 for that matter.

There are not only more sellers, but there are more buyers with $1,000-4,000 for down payments in the low-end than there are with large down payments for the more expensive properties.

I perceive this situation as a pyramid shape. Most of the investors can only afford the cheaper properties. They are at the base of the pyramid. As you go higher in price, the volume of buyers begins to thin out. Once you reach the top where you find the most expensive properties, there is virtually no one there. Therefore, there is a greater supply of sellers and buyers in the cheaper properties. This reality makes this investment opportunity most desirable.

Based on my success, I recommend purchasing properties $10-20,000 under market and in the $20,000 price range that are habitable or near habitable that do not require large sums of cash to bring them to city code standards. These standards create a neat, clean, and safe environment, of which I agree. The whole idea, in a nutshell, is to purchase with low money down, make minimal repairs, and FAST-FLIP for a substantial **paper profit**.

Price Range Respective To Your Area.

My area of investment is in the older section of the inner-city of Columbus, Ohio. How does my pricing and rental amounts compare to investors in Los Angeles or elsewhere? In many cities the situation could be the same or cheaper. Based upon the information a former tenant has given me, the costs of both housing and rents are twice my figures in Los Angeles, though.

Suppose that my 3 bedroom double rents for $700 for both sides, but somewhere else it is $1400 for the same units in the same type of neighborhoods. Also, the average selling price of around $20,000 that I pay could also be increased to $40,000, for example. If your rents are twice my amount, you can easily conclude that with the additional $700 monthly rent you can pay much higher purchase prices than I do to accomplish the same goal, $40,000 for example.

To compensate for the higher cost of expenses and living you can simply create a note for $12,000 or more, instead of $10,000. It is all relative. Just calculate your buyer's conservative rate of return and insure that it remains above 20%. Keep in mind that the $20,000 purchase price can be just a rule of thumb for you. As long as you can acquire a note for $10,000, after getting your investment capital back, you have achieved your goal.

Neighborhoods.

You are looking to purchase properties in the older section of the inner-city. There are many neighborhoods to choose from and they are all unique and different. Some are certainly more worse than others. Although you will select a neighborhood that is predominately welfare and the residents work at low-end jobs, do select a decent neighborhood. Here you will find cheap, but salable, properties.

Unless you invest in just one or two buildings at a time, confine your purchases to one neighborhood. The repairs, management, and resale of your projects as a whole become easier with proper time management. Centralizing all properties at one location permits you to shave off excess travel time and attain a desirable comfort level in your workload.

Target Properties.

Smaller properties with assumable financing in the low-end of pricing in the low-income neighborhoods have served me best. Based upon my experience, the expense and profit projections are so outlined. (You can modify type, location, and price.)

Multi-units currently rented with long term and clean tenants are the perfect and ideal situations for the Fast-Flip, except for Plan V, where singles work best. (Admittedly, singles and even 12-unit buildings could be worked into the rest of the system. Upon selling existing portfolios, a whole host of properties could apply.)

After completing minor cosmetic improvements you can place these properties right back on the market with curb appeal and offer financing.

* OUTSIDE NICE / INSIDE NICE *

The majority of properties that you purchase will be fully occupied, but will be comprised of low rents, poor housekeeping, and will require a multiplicity of minor repairs.

The art of this strategy is to accurately gauge the financial expenditures required before any purchase is ever made. This ability will enable you to decide which properties do, and do not, fit into these programs. Once you have acquired this talent through experience, buying and selling with these techniques will become routine.

You're A Professional. Modify!

Conversely, if you have been cultivating an area where the neighborhood is nicer, $50-100,000 for example, and single homes are your forte, you can modify my techniques and reformulate the plans. It is really no different from my providing the ingredients and you adding to or slightly changing the recipe. You are a seasoned investor; you can even modify your own methods by adding my twists to improve your current strategies.

Contracts.

1. *Real Estate Purchase Contract.* Obtain one from your local Board of Realtors or Bar Association. Buy one and make copies yourself. (Office supply stores ordinarily do not offer an all inclusive and up-to-date form.) Use for buying and selling Plans I, II, and III. Also, use when buying V and selling Plan 1V.

2. *Option To Purchase Contract.*

Recommended when contracting to buy for Plan IV. You can instruct an attorney to draw up a standard form, and modify when needed. It is near impossible to locate a form to buy, unless you get lucky and find one in an office supplies store. However, for your con-venience, I have enclosed one applicable to Ohio at the end of Chapter 7. You will contract to buy with it, but sell with the standard real estate purchase contract.

3. *Rental Agreement W/Addendum.*

Use this when selling on the Lease With The Option To Purchase in Plan V. It is found in Chapter 8.

Real Estate Agents' Role.

With a total project input of $4,000, there is not much room for commission fees for buying and selling on a single project. Upon purchase, try to buy from owners directly, without agents.

Understandably, many acceptable properties will be listed with real estate agents.

Providing the deal is right, you can pay the buying commissions and sometimes even negotiate them down. If the listing agent or broker is also the selling agent or broker, all of the commissions are paid to that one company without a co-op fee; usually 7%. This enables either the listing agent, or broker, to have more room to bargain. Hopefully, they will find it more feasible to sell the property to you today and make a little less. The alternative is to wait longer for another buyer and risk losing the sale or listing altogether, making further advertising expenses in the process.

When you reach the point when you resell the property, most of the time could be without enlisting the services of real estate agents. This investment/residential property will be so easy to sell that even those of you with absolutely no experience could sell it in the Sunday newspaper under the investment section. You are offering a property with high rents and deposits in decent condition for $2,000-4,000 down at a reasonable price with an extremely high return. You will not need any help whatsoever to unload that type of property. It will sell itself. However, if you maintain agent contacts, like I do, a simple phone call may sell the property immediately. Speed is always a consideration.

Although real estate commissions are costly, agents can be a terrific asset in acquisitions. Provisions and adjustments have been made in the investment calculations to allow for such expenses. Even when selling, you can sometimes still do so through agents without exceeding the limitations.

Have Tenant Debt Assigned To You.

Often, tenants are not paying rent. Whenever possible, delay the closing until those units are vacant. The eviction costs and rent losses with this tactic will be incurred by the seller.

If that doesn't work and the tenant has a job, have the debt owed to the seller transferred to you in the initial contract offer. You can try to collect the back rent from a cooperative tenant and keep it for yourself.

At the very least, you can obtain a judgement for what is currently owed to you and the back rent owed to the seller and go for the garnishment. Strike a deal where you both participate in collections. After expenses, you could enter a 75/25 split, you being the 75%.

Shift Repairs To Seller.

Sometimes a chimney needs flashed, which may be a big project for you. When you mention it to the seller it may seem minor to him. During the contract offer is a great opportunity for you to have him make the repair before the closing takes place at no cost or a nominal one to you.

Whenever possible, shift as many of the repairs, closing costs, and commissions to the seller. This could save you a tidy sum.

Sell To Qualified Buyers.

Selling properties to buyers who do not pay is real discouraging and defeatist. Moreover, it is time consuming and expensive to foreclose on properties, take them back, make repairs, and then resell again.

Investors who put $2,000-4,000 who earn over $60,000 at jobs and investors with tons in real estate and income are your best buyers. Most of my buyers have fallen into these two categories.

Not all buyers will do this well, but it is not necessary. Buyers who pay their bills on time and can afford to make the investments with my required down payments are good enough for me.

On occasion, I encounter obnoxious sellers who state that they can possibly find an owner-occupant to pay $45,000 with nothing down and charge $600 per month on the payment for the same properties that I buy for $20,000. This is lunacy and those sellers will get much more than they bargain for with this attitude. Selling at rip-off prices to an owner-occupants without credit checks in these neighborhoods with nothing down are foreclosures just waiting to happen. The sellers think that they are taking advantage of the buyers, but even the buyers know who will ultimately get burned. Later, the seller will wish that he sold the property at a reasonable price to someone like me who really makes his payments. They would have saved money in the long run because now they must either fix the properties again or lower the prices even below what I would have paid before.

The key to creating notes is to create good notes that both the seller and buyer will respect and honor. Granted, anyone could lose their $30-60,000 per year position and even file bankruptcy. But odds are that this type of individual will survive and get something going to replace his lost income. In essence, quality notes are key to your success. Set good notes in motion, collect monthly, and forget about them. Then set more good notes in motion. Selling to the wrong buyer is truly a mistake.

Check Your State Laws.

Call your respective State Division of Consumer Finance, or attorney, to find out what financing methods are legal and which are not. Regardless of what I've done in Ohio, the laws could have since been changed by the time Ohioans have read this book. Furthermore, each state has its own laws and regulations and they do significantly differ from one state to another.

Is this a problem? It could require major renovation for Plan IV. But not in Plans I, II, III, or V, i.e., as long as you make the necessary phone calls to find out what is legal and what is not. Afterward, make the necessary adjustments.

Ask:

Can I originate first mortgages without a license?
If yes: One more option for you to choose from.

If no: Land Sales Contracts can be an alternative when
selling. Ask about the legality of those. It does have
many advantages.

What does it take to acquire the license to originate first
mortgages?

What if my seller originates a first mortgage for me? How
does it affect me as a buyer? Am I doing anything that
violates the law? If not, can I let my buyer assume the first
mortgage created for me by my seller if it is an assumable
loan?

Can I originate second mortgages without a license?

If yes: One more option for you to choose from.

If no: Assumable Land Sales Contracts, cognovit notes,
personal notes, and having a licensed company do
the paperwork for you are viable alternatives. If
you really feel the need for this option, get a
license.

Are **cognovit notes** legal in this state?

If yes: A good device when selling.

If no: Just avoid it.

Can I advertise a property for sale in the newspaper with
just an Option To Purchase Contract without having the
deed in my name or a Land Sales Contract?

If yes: Plan IV need not be modified.

If no: Plan IV requires serious modification.

Are Land Sales Contracts legal in this state?

If yes: A good device when selling.

If no: Plan V needs major restoration. Eliminate it as a
viable alternative in all plans.

What is the maximum interest rate allowable for:
                              1st   2nd   3rd mortgages?

An individual can charge another individual is:
                    ____% ____% ____%

A corporation can charge an individual is:
                    ____% ____% ____%

A corporation can charge a corporation is:
                    ____% ____% ____%

An individual can charge a corporation is:
                    ____% ____% ____%

This short Q and A inquiry will automatically steer you in the right direction. When I discuss second mortgages and you are forbidden to utilize them, substitute an alternative financing method, such as a personal note or Land Sales Contract. The examples are quite receptive to changes. (Also feel free to interject cognovit notes, when applicable.)

For example, if you are forbidden to advertise a property for sale in the newspaper in your state (unless it is done through a real estate broker, or by the deed holder of a property) it drastically affects the livelihood of Plan IV. This creates a problem because you advertise in my plan with only the Option To Purchase, not the deed. It does not totally kill the plan, rather makes it difficult to function effectively and swiftly. However, if you have contacts in a real estate investment organization, or have a superb client list, this plan may still be viable. However, I would call to get all the specifics of what is and is not permitted in your respective state regarding the Option To Purchase.

CHAPTER 2

FAST-FLIP FOR
NOTE ACCUMULATION

Plan I: Overall Objectives.

Simply, you assume loans, limit your cash investment to $4,000 per project, sell to get your cash back, and create notes payable to yourself for $10,000 each. It sounds easy and it is, providing that you adhere to my guidelines and instructions.

At first, set yourself a realistic goal of accumulating 10 notes payable for 10 years for $10,000 each totaling $100,000. Upon doing so, you have mastered this plan and should set yourself a new goal of $500,000, and afterward a goal of $1 million.

Since Plan I involves a quick resale strategy, depreciation is not a consideration. In fact, cash flow does not play an integral role in your final profit picture either. Since cash flow is important to your buyers, you will calculate your projected cash flow based upon rental increases after purchase, which aids in calculating your buyer's projected cash flow. This conservative slant in calculations has been added to allow for mistakes.

Investors who engage other full time careers will find two simultaneous real estate projects to be sufficient. However, the full time real estate investors' only limitations will be their own time management abilities and financial capabilities.

Expense Projections.

Your project expenses can be easily broken down and charted into three categories to simplify for analysis: buying, repairing, and selling costs. Even before the property is purchased, you will set a total project dollar limitation of $4,000. The three categories can fluctuate in amounts, but totaled cannot exceed the $4,000 limit. This $4,000 figure is based on your buyer's highest down payment. Based upon my experience of buying and selling, it is quicker to sell with owner-financing of $4,000 or less. In fact, as you lower the down payment you can raise the selling price, thereby increasing the field of buyers and selling the property much quicker.

Maximum Total Project Expenses

Buying Costs	Repair Costs	Selling Costs	Job Total
$ 500	$3,000	$ 500	$4,000
-$ 500	$3,500	$1,000	$4,000
$1,000	$2,000	$1,000	$4,000

The above figures are based on and determined by what the buying, repairing, and selling costs could total. Note that each proposed project in all three categories does not exceed the $4,000 self imposed limitation. Acknowledging this, the categories and their respective figures must be examined before the purchases are made.

You can play an active roll in reducing the buying, repairing, and selling costs to maintain your maximum dollar input of $4,000 by shifting costs to the seller and account receivables to yourself discussed in Chapter 1.

Calculating The Rate Of Return: Conservative Vs. Aggressive.

Sometimes it is better to perceive the project as what it will be when you sell it rather than what it is now when you are buying it. Once I bought a three bedroom per side double where the rent on one side was $125 and the other side was vacant. If I had put this rent roll to any formulas and based my decision on them I would certainly not have invested in it. However, I based my decision upon what the investment would be after my changes were implemented.

By the same token, upon buying the property your focus should be on the next step as well, selling. You need to perceive and predict what your buyer will perceive the investment to be. The problem I have with many sellers is that they are unrealistic. Sellers should compute and formulate the deal they expect someone else to buy. It should be a good deal with a good return.

This is what *you* will do. The property will be a good deal for you when you buy it, and will also be a good deal for your buyer when he buys it.

The conservative rate of return calculation is figured by subtracting an additional 30% from the monthly rental income to allow for a vacancy and maintenance allowance. This also allows for mistakes in rental projections and unpredictable repairs and expenses. This is the approach and outlook that I recommend you focus upon whenever ROR calculations are made for Plans I, II, and III. Plan IV needs projections only to establish a selling price because there is virtually nothing for you to lose except time and small advertising fees. Plan V should show at least a 20% Rate Of Return for you for the first 3 years. Since a homeowner will buy, rental projections are not applicable to the buyer.

The aggressive rate of return is one where the 30% vacancy and maintenance expense allowance has not been calculated. Many buyers under-calculate their return because they are good at minimizing expenses by not making any repairs unless it is absolutely necessary. When repairs are made, they will go to great lengths to patch, rather than replace.

Both calculations will be provided throughout the examples because I want you to see *your* calculation, conservative, and their calculation, aggressive. Some calculations are projections and others are directly from my tax returns.

On actual case histories, the conservative rates of return do not reflect the 30% vacancy allowance, rather actual figures from the projects themselves are used. The conservative rate of return will, on these examples, reflect face value, or current balance, of notes. Conversely, the aggressive approach will then reflect notes as if they were to fully pay out for the term of the note.

When it comes to note values, I prefer to perceive them aggressively, as if they fully pay out. To me, this is their true value. Ordinarily, you will find me on the conservative side of the fence. Both are outlined for you to examine.

*** **Rate Of Return Formulas** ***

Annual Cash Flow ÷ Amount Invested =
Annual Rate Of Return

(Project Cash Flow ÷ Amount Invested) ÷ Years Owned =
Aver. Annual Project Cash Flow(or Rate Of Return)

(Project Net ÷ Amount Invested) ÷ Years of Return
= Average Annual Project Rate Of Return

(Note Income ÷ Amount Invested) ÷ Yrs of Return
= Annual Note Rate Of Return

Conservative Vs. Aggressive ROR

Cash flow :
Conservative = Rents - (PITI + 30% Rents)
Aggressive   = Rents - PITI

Note Value:
Conservative = Face value, or balance of note due.
Aggressive   = Income when fully paid out.

EXAMPLE 2A

A. When You Buy.

As I stated, you cannot accurately assess your buying position and project profits with any formulas based upon existing low rents. This is a good opportunity to acquire a good deal. The rents and deposits might be low and the seller need not be currently experiencing a large cash flow for you to make the purchase. If the seller did have a higher monthly cash flow, he would surely expect a higher price for the property. For whatever reason, some landlords are incapable of raising rents. As a buyer, this is to your advantage because you will raise rents and deposits. (Deposits are increased on new tenants only.)

You could increase rents to $350 per side and insert those figures into my formula. Ordinarily, you take the yearly income minus all expenses divided by your cash down payment and you will find the rate of return. However, even the aggressive rate of return calculated throughout this book includes the property's first 90 days repair costs added to the down payment in the amount invested figure. By computing this way, the aggressive calculation in these circumstances have a conservative slant.

Your plan is to limit your investment cash to $4,000 and try to keep purchase prices under $20,000. Granted, often you can purchase for $18,000 and repair for $2,000 but the example below illustrates the purchase price of $20,000 with $1,000 down and an additional $2,500 in repairs and calculates that rate of return. In the final analysis, it does not matter whether you pay $20,000 or $30,000. Likewise, it doesn't significantly matter if the note is $8,500 or $11,500.

Balance after down pmt.	$19,000	Monthly Rents	$700
Cash amt. invested (Dn. pmt. & immed. repairs)	$ 3,500	Est. Mo. PITI	-$260
		30% Vac. And Maint.	-$210
		Monthly Cash Flow	**$230**

Monthly cash flow $230 X 12
= $2,760 Annual Cash Flow

Annual Cash Flow ÷ Amount Invested
= Rate Of Return
$2,760. ÷ $3,500. = 79% Conservative ROR
$5,280. ÷ $3,500. = 151% Aggressive ROR

Upon initial calculations and projections, do include your estimated immediate repair costs and a 30% vacancy and maintenance allowance in your cash flow to allow for a very conservative calculation to provide a wide margin for error.

From the typical investor's standpoint, the additional 30% is not calculated, nor are the immediate repairs. For the average investor who will buy your investment property, I will calculate the proverbial perception of how to calculate the rate of return with the buyer's maximum $4,000 down payment and without the 30% deduction, nor any immediate repairs. That figure will be the aggressive calculation positioned directly below the conservative figure.

The reality is that you will not own the property for a year and you will not actually experience these returns based on annual returns. Rather they will be higher because of only a three month investment period. But to properly evaluate properties for yourself and realistically project your buyers' calculations you will perform the calculations to comfortably predict your buyers' perceptions and project outcomes.

Your turn-around-time from buying to selling will be within 90 days and you will get all of your $3,500 back, creating a mortgage note payable to you for $10,000. In actuality, this would be your return. Your goal on every deal is to get your cash input back right away with a mortgage note for $10,000.

B. When You Sell.

Your tremendous and realistic cash flow sets up a good deal for your buyer. With this deal you may need an additional $500 for closing costs to sell the property. The total you have now invested would be $4,000. If so, your buyer would need $4,000 down to replenish your cash reserve.

On many occasions, your buyer will need only $2,000-3,000, and this is even better. The lower you make the down payment, the quicker you find a buyer. Your buyer's down payment depends primarily upon your own cash input.

(In Plan IV, Chapter 7, my buyers' down payments were only $1,000.) By now you have the property in good repair, and from a buyer's standpoint, its appearance and income are quite impressive. When your buyer begins his calculations there are no water bills to include because of sub-metering. The taxes are low because of the low selling prices. The rents have also been increased to $700 per month. Plug these figures and your $10,000 note into the Rate Of Return Formula and see what your buyer discovers.

Your Buyer's Analysis			
1st Mortgage	$19,000	Mo. PITI	$260
2nd Note you Create	$10,000	Mo. Payment	$132
Contract Down Pmt.	$ 4,000	Total Mo. Pmt.	$392
		Mo. Rental Income	$700
		Buyer's PITI	-$392
		30% Vac. and Maint.	-$210
Total	$33,000	Buyer's Cash Flow	$ 98

Monthly cash flow $98 X 12
= $1,176 Annual cash flow

$1,176 ÷ $4,000 = 29% Conservative ROR

(Monthly cash flow W/O 30%) $308 X 12
= $3696 Annual cash flow

$3,696 ÷ $4,000 = 92% Aggressive ROR

Your buyers do not find deals like this very often. Will they squabble about the added

$10,000? Not hardly. Investors perceive returns above 20% as successful. If your buyer does not utilize the conservative 30% vacancy and maintenance allowance in his computation his return will be 92%.

Now that you have a knowledge base and understand the fundamentals and objectives of Plan I, it is time to continue with the specifics of the program and its applications. Chapters 3 and 4 further detail Plan I.

CHAPTER 3

FAST-FLIP
FHA AND VA ASSUMABLE LOANS

Plan I.

FHA and VA assumptions will be your bread and butter. The bulk of your deals will be of this variety. So learn the specifics well. FHA and VA loans you assume are easy and quick loans to close, second only to assuming Purchase Money Mortgages. There is absolutely no qualifying on many of them. Check the loan origination date to determine assumability requirements, as discussed in Chapter 1.

You can modify Plan I to become a SLOW-FLIP by simply landlording and selling much later. All examples, though, are FAST-FLIP.

Simple Assumptions.

If a seller just wants to unload the property without a real estate agent and not receive any money at closing, you will experience a very basic closing. Once the purchase price is established, all that will be negotiated is who will pay for the title insurance and closing fees. Ordinarily, the seller will bring the real estate taxes up to date, pro-rate rents, return deposits, pay for title insurance, and pay for most of the closing costs.

For example, if the purchase price is $17,000 and you buy directly from the seller, your fees will be vary slightly depending on the closing agent, but will be quite small just the same. In some cases, the seller will bring money to the closing table and you will leave with some.

When buying, time the closing on the 10th of the month after the rents have been collected. If the rents are $250 per side, they total $500 per month. Since your closing is on the tenth, 2/3 of this amount belongs to you. However, 2/3 of the payment is yours as well because the assumption of the mortgage is generally immediate. Regardless, the rents should exceed the payment and you come out ahead at closing.

On examples of 3A through 3D, I have detailed buyer and seller expenses to show the general cost breakdown. To study or review detailed closing costs in future chapters refer back to this beginning section. As you progress through the examples, the detailing and focus will be on different specifics, rather than belaboring closing details.

EXAMPLE 3A

You can shave off the title insurance and closing fee entirely if you can convince your seller to pay for them. Ordinarily, sellers do cover these costs because your down payment is more sizable and the costs are simply deducted from that down payment. But in a "nothing down" situation, like this one, it becomes more difficult. However, if the seller is motivated enough, he may make the concession to cover the costs entirely or even split them.

In some of your buying situations, though, there are vacancies, someone is not paying rent, or there are no deposits.

When You Buy W/O Agent.

Original Loan Amount $25,000 For 30 Years		
Current Loan Balance Of 1st Mortgage $17,000. PI $201.16 @ 9%		
12 Years Remaining. Purchase price $17,000.		
Title Insurance	$ 87.50	Arbitrary figure
Assumption Fee	$125.00	
Closing Fees	$385.00	
Partial 2/3 of PI	$134.11	
Total	$731.61	Plus a $17,000 mortgage
Rent Credit	-$333.33	
Tax Proration Cred.	-$300.00	
Rental Deposits	-$500.00	
Total Down payment	+$401.72	Credit you take home

Consequently, the figures above could reflect you putting money down, rather than leaving with some.

If a real estate agent is involved, you will add about 7% to the figures above. Based on a selling price of $17,000 the commission would be $1,190. Some companies charge 10% on low-end properties. Others have a minimum commission fee from $1,000 to $2,500.

When You Buy W/Agent.

Buying Credit	+$ 401.72
7% Commission	-$1,190.00
Total Down payment	-$ 788.28

Granted, this puts a monkey wrench in your works. However, your volume and productivity is significantly increased by utilizing real estate agents. This deal would truly be worth the $1,190 fee. Although the fee is $1,190, you still only need $788.28 at the closing because your credits offset some of the cost.

Often, the agent will state that $2,000 down will make the deal work. Although this is a good deal, you can make it better. When the seller just wants to unload, calculate expenses to the penny. Why pay more than necessary? The purchase price could total the loan balance, some closing costs, and the sales commission. (The closing costs you and the seller will each pay should be carefully spelled out.)

Furthermore, if you act nonchalant you might even get the agent or broker to reduce his commission. If you act a slight bit interested, you will not only pay the full commission but may even pay a higher price as well. For the most part, agents represent sellers. Moreover, they represent themselves. In most cases, agents receive a higher commission as the sales price increases. In essence, if you pay an additional $1,000 the agent can make another whopping $35-70, based upon a 7% sales commission. It seems amazing that he will burn you for an additional $1,000 so that he can make $70, but it could happen. It is his job to get as much for the seller as he possibly can, thereby increasing his income in the process. To prevent this situation, you must act disinterested, even while the contract offer is being written. It is a game. The key is to convince the agent and seller that you are willing to cover some expenses only. With practice, your performances during negotiations could be brilliant, and you win by paying less. Consider the savings on just one deal. Consider the savings on all your deals as a whole!

After completing the necessary repairs for resale, put it up for sale immediately. Your buyer's down payment will consist of reimbursing yourself for your own down payment, plus the $1,500-2,000 in your repair expenses. In addition, your buyer will pay $10,000 on a note, possibly secured by a second mortgage payable to you. Your buyer will pay you $132.16 PI for 10 years at 10%. This is your profit.

To sell, have the closing at the end of the month, the last day if possible. (I'm assuming that the rents exceed the payment.) This eliminates the necessity to pro-rate rents. Have your note begin on the first, following the closing date, even if it is just one day.

Also, please note that, in this example, the rents and deposits have since been raised to $350 per unit on a 2-unit building.

As I illustrated, you bought the property with a credit of $401.72 w/o agent. Now, add the selling credit of $1,615 to the buying credit. This totals $2,016.72. You have no cash of your own in the project except for repair costs, which can equal the total amount you received between buying and selling. Typically, you will

When You Sell W/O Agent.

Contract Down Payment $3,000.00			
Summary Of Buyer's Trans.		**Summary Of Seller's Trans.**	
Gross Amt. Due From Buyer		Gross Amt. Due To Seller	
Contract Price	$30,000.00	Contract Price	$30,000.00
Buyer's Fees	$ 65.50		
Gross Due From Buyer	**$30,065.50**	**Gross Due Seller**	**$30,000.00**
Paid By/For Buyer		Reductions To Seller	
1st Mtge.	$17,000.00	1st Mtge.	$17,000.00
2nd Note	$10,000.00	2nd Note	$10,000.00
Rental Deposits	$ 700.00	Rental Deposits	$ 700.00
County Taxes	$ 300.00	County Taxes	$ 300.00
		Closing Costs	$ 385.00
Total Pd. By/For Buyer	**$28,000.00**	**Total Reductions**	**$28,385.00**
Gross Amt. Due From Buyer	$30,065.00	Gross Due Seller	$30,000.00
Less Amt. Due From Buyer	$28,000.00	Less Reductions	$28,385.00
Cash From Your Buyer	**$ 2,065.00**	**Cash To Seller**	**$ 1,615.00**

be subtracting buying costs from selling credits. If the expenses equal this total credit you are right on target in reimbursing yourself for all costs involved with the project, and earning a mortgage note for $10,000. If your total allows for extra cash profit now, good for you.

Realistically, you may reduce the buyer's down payment and increase the note amount. For example, if your total invested is only $2,016.72 and the repairs were funded out of the cash flow you could have a much lower down payment down, reducing the $4,000 to $2,000. This could increase the note from $10,000 to $11,000, thereby increasing the monthly payment to you from $132.16 to $145.22. This logic is not so much to enhance the monthly income, as it is to unload the property faster. As I stated earlier: the lower the down payment, the quicker the sale.

Also, I illustrated this example using a real estate agent. $788.28 was required to purchase this same piece of property. This time, though, subtract $788.28 from the selling credit of $1,615 This total of $826.72 gives a somewhat different look. There is not the flexibility to reduce your buyer's down payment, nor to increase repair expenses. It is not a real threat, though, because the numbers still work good, except that your buyer's down payment will need to be closer to $4,000. You only need to be more diligent and precise with the numbers and conscientious of repair expenses.

Now I am sure that you are wondering how to figure all this after the contracts and closings are completed and the project is sold. Well, you don't. You must do calculating before the offer is even made. Whether or not you utilize a real estate agent affects the repair expenses and reflects on what you require on your buyer's down payment.

More importantly, you need to calculate buying and selling expenses to determine how they affect your repair costs. You can more accurately gauge repair expenses as you gain further experience.

The figures and detailed information above enable you to compare your potential projects to them and predict the outcome of your investment even before your investment is made. Calculate and estimate buying, repairing, and selling expenses, then adjust the figures to make it work with your seller and your potential buyer. If the numbers do not balance cancel your plan for purchasing.

Buying Credit $401.72 + Selling Credit $1,615
= $2,016.72

($2,016 received + $10,000 Note) - Repairs of
($2,016) = Profit

$10,000 Note = Profit = Goal

In essence, as long as the repairs, in this case, have not exceeded the credits of $2,016.72 you have achieved your goal. The gist of the plan is to get your money back and get a mortgage note. If your repairs were at $1,500, you can either lower your buyer's down payment or profit-take the difference between $1,500 repair money and $2,016.72 in cash you received.

However, if you utilized a real estate agent, as in this example, your buyer will need an additional $1,190. Simply add the $1,190 to your other costs of $2,016.72 to figure your buyer's new down payment. In either case, there is still room for additional repairs because the buyer's down payment is still below $4,000.

$2,016.72 Buyer's Minimum Down Payment
Without Agent

$2,016.72 + $1,190 = $3,206.72
(Buyer's Minimum Down Payment With Agent)

With agents, your investment still remains low, but does not allow for much margin for adjustments in repairing, buying, and selling costs.

Regardless of whether you had spent $1,190 in real estate commissions as in the second part of Example 3A, or not, as in Examples 3B through 3D forthcoming, there are adequate profits here in both type of these examples. The main idea here is to add whatever costs you incurred during this endeavor to the buyer's down payment and keep his down payment as low as possible.

Is this a good deal for most investors? Granted, your buyer is paying $30,000 for a property in good repair with a small down payment, but will the investment earn him a satisfactory return? Examine the figures below.

Regardless of the method of calculation, you will find very eager investors to purchase this property. Whoever gets this deal will be quite pleased with himself. Even the most calculating of investors, so to speak, will savor this investment.

Your Buyer's Analysis.

1st Mtge.	$17,000	Mo. Pmt.	$201.16
2nd Note	$10,000	Mo. Pmt.	$132.16
Contract Dn Pmt	$ 3,000		
Your Buyer's PI			**$333.32**
Total	$30,000	Taxes and Ins.	$ 50.00
		Your Buyer's PITI	**$383.32**
		Mo. Rental Income	$700.00
		Your Buyer's PITI	$383.32
		30% Vac. & Maint.	$210.00
		Mo. Cash Flow	**$106.68**

Annual Cash Flow ÷ Amount Invested
= Rate Of Return

$1,280.16 ÷ $2,016.72 W/O Agent
= 63% Conservative ROR

$3,800.16 ÷ $2,016.72 W/O Agent
= 188% Aggressive ROR

$1,280.16 ÷ $3,206.72 W/Agent
= 40% Conservative ROR

$3,800.16 ÷ $3,206.72 W/Agent
= 119% Aggressive ROR

The pleasure will be all yours though. Think of the magic of no taxes, insurance, maintenance, vacancies, no.........tenants. Yet, you get a payment month after month, year after   year.

Assuming Low Balance Mortgages.

As these mortgage balances reduce, so increases their likelihood that someone will place a second mortgage upon them. Providing that you reach the seller before someone else does, this will be a great opportunity for you. Unfortunately, if the loan balance is $10,000 and the selling price is $20,000, the seller generally has his sights set on $10,000 minus expenses. The good news is that not many investors are willing to put $10,000 down on small inner-city properties. After a couple of months of the property sitting on the market, the seller will realize that he will either negotiate a better deal for a buyer or end up keeping the property himself.

EXAMPLE 3B

With assumptions, you negotiate the deal down to $17,500. Assume the existing 1st mortgage balance of $10,000 with the PI payment of $149.20 and the remaining term of about 10 years. However, there is a difference of $7,500 that you still need to pay the seller.

As I explained, your own down payment will generally vary from a $500 credit to $2,000. And, you want to factor all expenses out to save every dollar. However, to avoid the repetitious closing costs and to simply illustrate the technique it will require precise figures.

The contract down payment is $2,000. Finance the balance of $5,500 through the seller. The seller can take back a 2nd mortgage

@ 8% for 10 years @ $66.74 PI per month. Assume that you spent another $1,500 on repairs.

When You Buy W/O Agent.

Assume 1st Mtge. Bal.	$10,000	Mo. Pmt.	$149.20
Original Bal.. $17,000		Taxes and Insur.	$ 50.00
Create 2nd Note	$ 5,500	Mo. Pmt.	$ 66.74
Contract Down Pmt.	$ 2,000	Your Mo. PITI	$265.94
Repairs	$ 1,500	Mo. Rental Inc.	$700.00
Purchase Price	$17,500	Your Mo. PITI	-$265.94
You Owe	$15,500	30% Vac. & Mnt.	-$210.00
		Mo. Cash Flow	$224.06

$2,688.72 ÷ $3,500 = 77% Conservative ROR
$5,208.72 ÷ $3,500 = 149% Aggressive ROR

You will make two payments every month. With the rents at $250 per side at the time of your purchase, you could easily resell this property quite quickly with very little work and get a $5,000 note. However, you want a $10,000 note. Make the most of this project. Get those rents and deposits increased from $250 to $350 per side, like I did in this example. Prospective buyers will easily justify your higher asking price based on that added cash flow of $200 per month and cosmetic improvements.

Your buyer will assume both the 1st mortgage that your seller created for you and the second mortgage which you created. Now you will create a 3rd mortgage for $10,000 @ 10% for 10 years with a monthly payment of $132.16, which your buyer will make to you. In essence, your buyer will owe and pay on three mortgages, or one mortgage and two notes. He will also have a down payment of around $3,500 to cover your own down payment and repairs. Remember, you want to get all of your cash back.

When You Sell W/O Agent.

1st Mtge.	$ 10,000	Mo. Pmt.	$149.20
2nd Note	$ 5,500	Mo. Pmt.	$ 66.74
Create 3rd Note	$ 10,000	Mo. Pmt.	$132.16
3-Note Balances	**$25,500**	Your Buyer's Mo. PI	$348.10
Purchase Price	$ 29,000	Est Taxes & Ins.	$ 50.00
Down Payment	$ 3,500	**Your Buyer's PITI**	**$398.10**
Real Estate Fees	$ 0	Mo. Rental Inc.	$700.00
		Your Buyer's PITI	$398.10
		30% Vac. & Maint	$210.00
		Mo. Cash Flow	**$ 91.90**

$1,102.80 ÷ $3,500 = 32% Conservative ROR
$3,622.80 ÷ $3,500 = 104% Aggressive ROR

Many investors might even perceive this investment with a 104% ROR, discounting the vacancy and maintenance allowance. However, this conservative technique permits you to make your investments desirable to all potential investors, regardless of their calculation methods, and allows you to make some level of error and still achieve you goal of a $10,000 note.

This is the essence of this program. You create the environment for selling the property at the time you are buying it. You must figure all of your out of pocket expenses because you want it all back from your buyer's down payment. Calculate all monthly payments that your prospective buyer will be expected to pay. If your buyer's down payment is above $4,000, or your own PITI payments upon purchasing do not allow for about $200 per month conservative cash flow, on a 2-unit, upon purchase to allow for the reduction your buyer will experience, either forget the deal or renegotiate. Either restriction which you set for yourself will disqualify the potential property. Your project must be attractive to potential buyers.

Wrapping Mortgages.

Another way to sell FHA and VA loan assumptions is to wrap all of the mortgages into one note and sell on Land Sales Contract, detailed here, or on a Mortgage Wrap, as detailed in Chapter 5. On FHA, VA, and PMM loans that are legally assumed, there will be no *due on sale* clauses, unless there is a side agreement with the seller and yourself. Stick with these. Don't integrate non-assumable mortgages in any of the programs.

If the current interest rate that you can charge is higher than the existing loan rate of the assumption, you can wrap the existing loan or loans with your new note and generate a little more profit off of the interest difference. This adds another dimension to the resale of your properties.

EXAMPLE 3C

Part 1: Assumption Method. (Based upon Ex. 3A)

Rents	$ 700			
1st Mtge.	$17,000	@ 9% =	$201.16	for 12 Years
2nd Note	$10,000	@ 10% =	$132.16	10 Yrs Pd to you
Note Totals	$27,000		$333.32	PI
			$ 50.00	TI
			$383.32	**Buyer's PITI**

$1,280.16 ÷ $2,016.72= 63% Conserv. ROR

$3,800.16 ÷ $2,016.72 = 188% Aggress. ROR

Part 2: Wrap Method.

Mtge.	$27,000	@12% =	$324.06	PI for 15 Years
			$ 50.00	TI
			$374.06	Buyer's Wrap PITI
			-$383.32	Buyer's Asm. PITI
			-$ 9.26	**Pmt. is dec. 10 yrs.**

$1,391.28 ÷ $2,016.72= 69% Conserv. ROR

$3,911.28 ÷ $2,016.72 = 194% Aggress. ROR

Notice that when your buyer does his new calculations that his rate of return increases by 6% after utilizing the wrap. The change is a subtle one which benefits both sides: more cash flow for the buyer and more long term income for you.

In Part 1 the buyer will make two payments: one to your seller on the 1st mortgage and one to you ;on your note. In Part 2, the buyer makes one smaller total payment to you, and you make your payment on the 1st mortgage to your seller, keeping the difference. However, in some instances the buyer can make the payment directly to your seller and another one to you, just like an actual assumption. This is only done with a very strong buyer.

In Part 1 of Example 3C, as with Example 3A, your monthly income from your note only lasts for 10 years. The monthly wrap changes are a decrease of $9.26 for 10 years totaling a decrease of $1,111.20, an increase of $122.90 for 2 years equaling $2,949.60, and an increase of $324.06 for an additional 3 years totaling $11,666.16. With just this simple adjustment you will increase your profit schedule from $15,859.20 to an additional $13,504.56 making the new profit total $29,363.76!

In other words, your buyer pays a total of $44,826.24 in Part 1, and a total of $58,330.80 in Part 2. The lower payment schedule increases the monthly cash flow and makes buying it more appealing to most buyers. The extended payment period goes quite unnoticed by your buyer. At first, the change appears to be quite minute and hardly worth the trouble. As you can see, this one project has become as lucrative as two.

The explanation for this huge discrepancy is because there was only 12 years left on a 30 year mortgage on a loan of a larger original amount. The loan had already been paid on for eighteen years and the payments made roll heavily into paying off the principle rather than going toward the interest. However, if you assume a loan that is new in existence, there is not that significant of an advantage to wrapping loans because the bulk of the payments made still go toward the interest.

Wraps do not work as effectively if an existing loan has 22 years remaining. You can hardly finance the project for only 15 years. You should at least hold the mortgage for that 22 years, which is fine. Carry the loan as least as long as the mortgage term, or do not wrap. Although the payment to you is reduced as the term extends, you want the income as lengthy as possible. This is your strategy. As the loan term lengthens, so does the time it takes for principle portions of your payment to exceed the interest portion. If your buyer pays a 30 year loan off after making payments for 5 years, he will virtually owe the entire originating balance.

EXAMPLE 3D

Part 1: Assumption Method.

Rents	$ 700			
1st Mtge. Bal.	$10,000	@10%=	$149.20	For 10 Years remaining
2nd Note Bal.	$ 5,500	@ 8% =	$ 66.74	For 10 Years
3rd Note Bal.	$10,000	@10%=	$132.16	For 10 Years
Note Totals	$26,790		$348.10	PI
			$ 50.00	TI
			$398.10	**Buyer's PITI**

$1,102.80 ÷ $3,500 = 32% Conservative ROR
$3,622.80 ÷ $3,500 = 104% Aggressive ROR

Part 2: Wrap Method.

1st Mtge Bal	$26,790	@12%	$384.36	PI for 10 Years
			$ 50.00	TI
			$434.36	Buyer's Wrap PITI
			-$398.10	Buyer's Asmp PITI
			$ 36.26	New pmt increases

$667.68 ÷ $3,500 = 19% Conservative ROR

$3,622.80 ÷ $3,500 = 91% Aggressive ROR

This wrap example provides a 13% lower rate of return for your buyer than the straight assumption method, but it will not deter your him from this project because it far exceeds the 20% standard investment goal set by many investors, even with the conservative figures.

The benefit return from wrapping here is increased by $36.26 per month for 10 years equaling an increase of $4,351.20, spread over the life of the loan. It is worth the extra effort.

CHAPTER 4

FAST-FLIP
PURCHASE MONEY MORTGAGES

Plan I.

Purchase Money Mortgages arise from a seller having a property free-and-clear of mortgages and liens. The seller provides owner financing and gives the buyer a first mortgage. These mortgages are not assumable if the mortgage so states that it is not assumable. If the mortgage does not address the assumability issue at all, then attorney's on both sides have an argument. And, of course, if the mortgage states that it is assumable, then it is. You can either create a new PMM for yourself or assume an existing PMM, just like FHA and VA loans.

PMM's You Originate.

Upon initiating a new PMM from a seller, have the preparer insert an assumability clause. This entire strategy only works with either no loans on it or loans which are assumable. Do not stray from this guideline.

Unlike the FHA and VA loans which are already established with the balance due, interest rate, and term of loan, a new PMM can be entirely initiated by you. You determine the loan specifics without a bank. Based upon your personal financial situation and current economic conditions, you can dictate the mortgage terms that are good for you right now and good for your buyer in three months from now.

Find out the interest rate that banks are charging on non-owner occupied investment properties and subtract one percent. This is the interest rate you and your buyer could agree upon. Further, if you are confident the market will bear higher rates, use them within your state's usury laws.

For my personal **keeper** owner financed properties I prefer to finance for 8 years. However, this significantly increases the payment and dramatically decreases the cash flow as well. When your buyer does his calculations for his rate of return with your added $10,000 it will either deter his purchase or possibly cause you to settle for a $5,000 note. That is why you will finance properties 10 to 30 years. The-longer-the-better to attain the lowest acceptable payment, getting the greatest return in the long run.

Understandably, I find 30 year notes ludicrous, but today's investors are brainwashed into believing that long term notes with a higher cash flow is smarter than short term notes with a lower cash flow. So cater to the **modern day buyer's mentality** and give them what they seek. However, with the low dollar figures you should settle at 5-15 year terms.

EXAMPLE 4A

Assume that the current investment lending interest rate is 11%. You will offer 8.5% and he counters at 9%. Your purchase price is $18,000 with a $1,000 down payment. You will specify note terms of $17,000 @ 9% for 15 years. The monthly principle and interest is $172.43 Add the estimated $50 taxes and insurance to obtain the PITI of $222.43.

When You Buy W/O Agent.

Rents	$ 700.00	
Purchase price	$18,000.00	
Down Payment	$ 1,000.00	
Original loan amount of	$17,000.00	@ 9% for 15 years
PI	$ 172.43	
PITI	**$ 222.43**	

Assume that all closing expenses remain constant and you would ordinarily leave the closing table with a credit of $401.72 as in Example 3A. However, this example calls for a $1,000 down payment. Rather than leave the closing table with a credit, you will bring $598.28. Also, assume that $2,000 was incurred in immediate repairs and rents total $700.

$3,210.84 ÷ $2,598.28= 124% Conserv. ROR
$5,730.84 ÷ $2,598.28= 221% Aggress. ROR

When You Buy W/Agent.

Costs	+$ 401.72	Credit
Down payment	-$1,000.00	
7% Commission	-$1,260.00	
Total down payment	**$1,858.28**	

$3,210.84 ÷ $3,858.28 = 83% Conserv. ROR
$5,730.84 ÷ $3,858.28 = 149% Aggr. ROR

As I mentioned earlier, you need to avoid real estate agent commissions whenever possible, but you will gladly pay commissions to acquire some deals, like this one.

After the property has been negotiated you can immediately compute the closing costs to estimate the repair expense allowance. You will back into it, so to speak. To begin calculations to figure the projected selling price, allow $3,858.28 (up to $4,000) for your cash input, add this to the 1st mortgage balance and a $10,000 note, which you create.

When You Sell W/O Agent.

Since the buyer did not actually put $4,000 down, your figures could be increased by $935. You can either estimate repair costs of $4,000 - $935, or have your selling contract specify that your buyer actually brings a cashiers check for the amount of $4,000 to the closing. If so, the **Cash From Your Buyer** would be $4,000.

Summary Of Buyer's Trans.		Summary Of Seller's Trans.	
Gross Amt. From Your Buyer		Gross Amt. Due To Seller	
Contract Price	$31,000.00	Contract Price	$31,000.00
Buyer's Fees	$ 65.50		
Gross fromBuyer	$31,065.50	Gross Due Seller	$31,000.00
Paid By/For Buyer		Reductions To Seller	
First Mortgage	$17,000.00	First Mortgage	$17,000.00
Second Note	$10,000.00	Second Note	$10,000.00
Rental Deposits	$ 700.00	Rental Deposits	$ 700.00
County Taxes	$ 300.00	County Taxes	$ 300.00
		Closing Costs	$ 385.00
Tot. Pd ByBuyer	$28,000.00	Tot. Reductions	$28,385.00
Gross from Buyer	$31,065.00	Gross Due Seller	$31,000.00
Less Amt. Due From Buyer	$28,000.00	Less Reductions	$28,385.00
Cash From Your Buyer	**$ 3,065.00**	**Cash Due Seller (You)**	**$ 2,615.00**

Buying Debit + Selling Credit = Closing Totals =
Repairs (-$1,858.28) + $2,615 = $756.72 =
Repairs

Maximum Down Payment = $4,000
$4,000 - $3,065 = $935 = Could increase
buyer's down payment $935 + $756.72 =
$1,691.72 = Maximum Repairs

Your Buyer's Analyses.

1st Mtge.	$17,000	Mo. Pmt	$172.43
2nd Note	$10,000	Mo. Pmt.	$132.16
Contract Dn Pmt	$ 4,000	Your Buyer's PI	$304.59
Purchase Price	$31,000	Est. Taxes And Ins.	$ 50.00
		Your Buyer's PITI	$354.59
		Mo. Rental Income	$700.00
		Your Buyer's PITI	$354.59
		30% Vac. and Maint.	$210.00
		Mo. Cash Flow	**$135.41**

$1,624.92 ÷ $3,065 = 53% Conservative ROR
$4,144.92 ÷ $3,065 = 135% Aggressive ROR

Even when your buyer puts $4,000 down, his ROR far exceeds 20%.

$1,624.92 ÷ $4,000 = 41 Conservative ROR

PMM's You Assume.

These mortgages are assumed quite similar to FHA and VA loan assumptions. However, you do not pay a $125 assumption fee, nor do you order a loan package from a lending institution. Otherwise, the conditions would virtually remain the same. You assume the conditions and terms of an existing loan.

This method itself is also identical to FHA and VA loan assumptions. You assume the 1st mortgage or 1st and 2nd mortgages, perform the necessary repairs, sell with the down payment equal to your cash input, and create a 2nd or 3rd note payable to you. If you again need the detailed information, refer back to Examples 3A through 3D.

CHAPTER 5

SELLING FHA, VA, and PMM'S: COMPLEX APPLICATIONS

Plan II: Delayed Note Returns (FAST-SELL).

Not always are deals clean and simple, culminating with a quick turnover. In some instances, you may want to keep and maintain a property for years before selling to obtain a note. If this was the case and you financed for a short term, it makes the payment difficult to work with using the techniques illustrated in the previous chapters. There are unorthodox methods you can implement to make these properties fit into the note mold. They are not as simplified as all the previous examples. Often you must wait a few years to receive a return. Properties in their final years of payoff that can be sold for more lengthier notes are best suited for the concepts in this chapter.

In 1993 I sold off many units to finalize my property consolidation phase. Within this grouping of buildings all over the inner-city were properties that I had planned to keep indefinitely. However, the acquisition of too many properties in too many areas made for poor time management and inefficiency. Consequently, I had many properties loan-free, and others with the short term high payment strategy, that I wanted to unload. Fortunately, all of these units were either loan-free or had assumable loans. This meant, of course, that I had the ability to carry all of the mortgages, not send my buyers to the bank, and sell the properties myself in a very short time frame.

Until now, you have acquired the basic knowledge to create notes in a systematic manner without intricate obstacles sometimes encountered in the real world. Below are two complex examples where PMM's existed on both deals whereby I permit one to be Wrapped and the other to be sold on a Land Sales Contract. Inside this chapter are secrets that will unfold that hold the answers to profit maximization on these type of notes where the profits initially appear to be very small, and even negative. In actuality, they were quite enormous after the final computations were made.

Applying Plan II to these projects, after following my basic philosophy of short term loans for quick payoffs, enabled me to obtain the full benefit from landlording as well as enjoy mortgage notes without any of the respon- sibilities. I do always maintain a large portfolio of properties to provide a consistent standard of living for myself. However, I also desire a large inventory of mortgage notes as well. This program gives me the best of both worlds. With Plan II, I can landlord for a few years and culminate the project with a mortgage note.

Since this method involves keeping properties for at least a couple of years, annual tax benefits and cash flow are considerations in your overall profit picture.

EXAMPLE 5A			

When I Bought W/O Agent.

On Dec. 1989, I purchased two doubles on one lot for $20,771.20 with a down payment of $527. My principle and interest payment was $318.01 @ 11% for 8 years and the rents were $1120 per month. This was indeed an unusual circumstance where the cash flow was so tremendous that it covered most of the repair costs. However, the first month of ownership, during December, did involve a loss on my tax return of $872.99 because of initial repairs. Therefore, this loss is added to the amount invested in order to follow the conservative thought..

When I Bought W/O Agent.

Purchase price	$20,771.20		
My down pmt.	$ 527.00	imm. repairs	$872.99
Monthly rents	$ 1120.00		
My PI	$ 318.01	@ 11%	for 8 yrs

$3,299.88 ÷ $1,399.99 = 236% Conserv. ROR
$8,689.88 ÷ $1,399.99 = 621% Aggr. ROR

While I Owned.

1990 Cash flow, after exp.	$1,239.99
$1,239.99 ÷ $1,399.99 =	89% Actual ROR
1991 Cash flow, after exp.	$4,176.14
$4,176.14 ÷ $1,399.99 =	298% Actual ROR
1992 Cash flow, after exp.	$5,195.51
$5,195.51 ÷ $1,399.99 =	371% Actual ROR
1993 Cash flow, after exp. (Sold 4-93)	$1,217.08
$1,217.08 ÷ $1,399.99 =	87% Actual ROR
1989-1993 Cash Flow Totals	$11,828.72
Mortgage Reduced Included in note	$ 6,175.62
Total Landlord Benefits	$18,004.34

(Project Cash Flow ÷ Amount Invested)
÷ Years Owned
= Average Annual Project Rate Of Return

($11,828.72 ÷ $1399.99) ÷ 3.25 Yrs. = 260%
Aver. Ann. Project ROR

Notice that depreciation was not calculated. As far as I am concerned, adding it in as profit and then subtracting it later is fruitless in these examples. My primary concern is realistic profits.

Landlording Assessment.

Note that my projected conservative rate of return was surpassed after I encountered the repairs in the first month, which is the way it should be. At first, my many repairs were costly to the cash flow, but at least I did not need to go into my savings to support the project. Regardless, all of my returns after the initial 30 days far exceeded the 20% level.

When I Sold W/O Agent.

Since I paid on this short term mortgage note for 3.25 years on a 8 year note, the balance reduced quickly. At the time of sale, the balance was down to $14,068.58. I offered this deal for a higher price of $45,000 to allow for negotiating on the down payment (higher asking price with a lower down payment), and to induce someone to buy other properties at a discount.

In order to unload another double for $35,000 to the same buyers on the Eastside with $5,000 down, I reduced both the selling price of this pair of doubles to $35,000, (together on one lot in Midtown) and the down payment to the buyer was a $647 credit. At the closing, I wrote a check for $1,168. My rental pro-rations of $522 that I collected right before the closing helped offset my selling deficit. Therefore, my selling loss at closing was actually only $646.

My buyer signed a note and mortgage for $33,180 payable with equal monthly installments of $328.54 @ 8% payable through April, 2007, which was 14 years. This meant that until the first mortgage payments of $318.01 expire in January 1998, I would actually receive only $10.53 per month for 57 months which only total $600.21. However, between February of 1998 and April of 2007, I will receive the entire $328.54 for 111 months totaling $36,467.94. My share of the note if fully paid out will net, with the $600.21, $37,068.15.

The interest rate at the selling time was so much lower than when I had purchased the property originally. I adjusted to the current economic conditions and to the selling of multiple properties by providing a rate of 8%, which was down from what I had bought earlier at 11%. If I had used the quick turnover method, it would not have been a problem. Unfortunately, by waiting 3.25 years and the interest rates moving downward in a record breaking manner, it cut into my profit schedule.

On the other hand, I did unload the property at a reasonable price. I enlarged the overall profit by paying down the 1st mortgage during my ownership by $6,175, which was originally $20,244.20, and I had a note payable to me for $33,180 @ 8%, whereby $19,111 @ 8% was really mine.

To the buyer's advantage, we figured the existing 11% mortgage in with the purchase price and he not only got my interest rate down to 8%, but he would pay 8% on my 1st mortgage of approximately $14,069 as well. Rather than the buyer assuming the 11% loan and paying me 8% on the balance his attorney thought he could outwit me out of a few dollars by gaining 3% there. Initially, it seemed so.

The counter attack to this strategy was that by the time I begin to receive my full payment on February 1998 his loan balance will be $25,766.43 and my first mortgage will be paid off. The reason for this is that the entire loan amount was wrapped totaling $33,180 for 14 years. After 57 more months, at the time of my payoff, the principle will not have come down much. The monthly interest paid even after those 57 payments would still exceed the amount going to the principle.

Consider my profit schedule if the property is sold again after 57 months when my note is due to payout and the balance due me at that time will be 25,766.43. (Today's investors are big into refinancing to obtain cash to buy more properties whenever there is a handful of equity). This method of structuring the loan strongly enhanced my profit potential.

My Buyer's Analysis.

Purchase Price	$35,000	My Buyer's PI	$ 328.54
14 Year Wrap Note	$33,180	My Buyer's PITI	$ 406.41
		Mo. Rental Income	$1120.00
		My Buyer's PITI	-$ 406.41
		30% Vac. And Maint.	-$ 336.00
	My Buyer's Mo. Cash Flow		**$ 377.59**

$4,531.08 ÷ -$547.20(Credit) = Infinite Consv.
ROR
$8,563.08 ÷ -$547.20(Credit) = Infinite Aggr.
ROR

Not so surprisingly, some prospective buyers drove by and were not interested. They wanted to own rentals that they could drive by with pride. Certainly, my buyer will be proud when completes his federal income tax return.

Since my buyers were investors of means, it was not a real threat to their livelihood that there are, in essence, two 1st mortgages. In a default situation, he could, arguably, be liable for the first mortgage of approximately $14,069 and his wrap of $33,180. In all my years of investing, this is a only time I encountered where the buyer chose this direction.

I'm not very impressed by the way his attorney set up the mortgages on this deal. This wasn't a Land Sales Contract, and it wasn't a second mortgage either. In essence, there were two 1st mortgages. I don't like it because, on paper, it looks as though he owes $14,069 on one mortgage and $33,180 on another. I will just assume that he felt safer with the deed and this arrangement than entering into a Land Sales Contract.

My Profit Summary.

I made 39 pmts. and there were 57 left on my 1st mortg. at resale.

Conservative Outlook		Aggressive Outlook	
Down payment	-$ 527.00	Down payment	-$ 527.00
Dec., 1989 loss	-$ 872.99	Dec., 1989 loss	-$ 872.99
Cash flow inc.	$11,828.72	Cash flow inc.	$11,828.72
Selling costs	-$ 646.00	Selling costs	-$ 646.00
Note face value	$33,180.00	Note if paid out	$55,194.72
Face 1st mortg.	-$14,069.00	1st if paid out	-$18,126.57
Net profit	**$28,893.73**	**Net profit**	**$46,850.88**

($28,893.73 ÷ $2,045.99)/3.25 Yrs = 435%
Aver. Ann. Project Consv. ROR

($46,850,88 ÷ $2,045.99)/14 Yrs = 164% Aver.
Ann. Project Aggr ROR

Contemplate that the project was bought for $20,771.20 and sold for $35,000. What would most people and investors figure that I made? Most would agree that you simply subtract one number from the other and deduce that $14,228.80 was the profit. My share of the note by itself, at closing, of $19,111 far surpasses that calculation by $4,882.20.

My argument would be that I did not make $14,228.80, rather I feel that I made over $35,000 on the sale alone. ($37,068.15 is my share of the note if fully paid out.) No one without reading the specifics would ever believe it!

Unfortunately, for this type of sale to be attractive, you need to be someone like myself who does not need money today and can delay the financial gratification for a few years. You cannot hardly survive and pay many bills with $10.53 per month. It appears to me, though, that if money were in dire need that either this property would have been sold for cash or a 2nd note would have been written for immediate income. As you recall, I did dramatically reduce the price and down payment to induce the buyer to purchase another double in another end of town. Therefore, the 2nd note would have been larger than in my case.

Neither at my time of purchase, nor at my time of selling, was a real estate agent used. This increased my profit and allowed for plenty of leeway for my buyer because I only had $1,399.99 of my money invested in the project. If I had utilized real estate agents, my buyer's down payment would have reflected that additional cash input. Furthermore, I speculate that the down payment would have been in the $4,000-6,000 range because of the two-double on one lot situation and a selling price in the low to mid $40,000's would have been required had I not wanted to unload that pesky double. This is to the buyer's credit. He found a seller who wanted to make this particular deal, me.

My Project Summary.

This was truly a rare occasion when the rate of return for cash flow was so astronomically high. The example itself involving different twists and delayed income were also quite unique as well.

Ordinarily, when wrapping a loan as described in Chapter 3, you increase the interest rate to enable you to pick up a few dollars on the existing 1st and/or 2nd mortgages and to run the term of loan on or about the term as the longest existing mortgage. However, the balance of the term on the first note consisted of only 4.75 years. Wrapping a loan of this short term caliber provided me with an added advantage. On June 1994, I began to pay off my 1st mortgage with the 2 to 1 principle to interest ratio reduction on my note. At the same time, his 1st mortgage ratio was 1 to 2 interest to principle ratio to me. In other words, since my 1st mortgage payments were near the end of its

8 year term, 2/3's of the payment went to the principle and increased with every payment. Since my buyer's term was 14 years, and we were at the very beginning, the interest then exceeded 2/3's of the first payment. It would take until September 2001 for my buyer to reach the point where 2/3's of his payment would go to his principle, rather than interest, like mine does now. This explains the magnitude of profit (equity) from my mortgage note.

If cash is needed and the buyer is willing, one twist that could have been implemented was a balloon payment. My buyer had already purchased another property from me 5 months earlier before contracting these two deals. On that particular deal we did have provisions for a large down payment of just over $20,000 and two subsequent $4,000 balloon payments @ 10% interest. He was one of those investors who did not fear balloon payments. We probably could have made provisions for a balloon payment somewhere in this note, perhaps after 4.75 years. I caution to burden an investor who is already on the hook for one balloon note to me. I want good quality notes for myself and excellent cash flow for my buyer. Anyway, with respect to my income taxes, I prefer long term notes to cash.

Again if I had not been pressured to unload that distant Eastside double, my profit schedule would have been increased by at least another $5,000, and possibly $10,000. However, sometimes your selling motives drive you to compromise your leverage, as it did mine here.

Selling FHA, VA, and PMM's

The compromise, though, will still yield me 164%!

EXAMPLE 5B

When I Bought W/Agent.

An even more bizarre situation and more complex for others to understand was my philosophy and strategy when in November, 1987 I bought 5 fee simple townhouses for $70,000. The seller took back 5 small mortgages totaling $60,000 @ 10% interest and a payment of $844.75 PI for 9 years. My actual down payment was $9,011.81. Soon after my purchase the rents were raised to $1,500 per month. My PITI on my PMM was $1,014.75.

PMM Purchase Price	$70,000.00	
Down Payment	$ 9,011.81	
PI	$ 844.75	@ 10% for 9 yrs.
PITI	$ 1,014.75	

$423 ÷ $9,011.81 = 5% Conservative ROR
$5,823 ÷ $9,011.81 = 65% Aggressive ROR

Landlording Assessment.

Landlording on this brick townhouse row was not exactly the highlight of my career. You might argue that my lackluster performance was caused to my high payment due to the short 9 year amortization. The fact of the matter is that when I finance it is almost always between 8 to 10 years. Arguably, this should have been financed for a longer term for most investors. I

94

do admit that even I should be careful as to how many alligators I own. However, this investment was totally turned around upon resale and has become one of my greatest triumphs, as you will soon see.

While I Owned.

1988 Cash flow, after exp.	$ 206.65
$206.65 ÷ $9,011.81 =	2% Actual ROR
1989 Cash flow, after exp.	$4,726.13
$4,726.13 ÷ $9,011.81 =	52% Actual ROR
1990 Cash flow, after exp.	$2,046.19
$2,046.19 ÷ $9,011.81 =	23% Actual ROR
1991 Cash flow, after exp.	-$1,343.80
(-$1,343.80) ÷ $9,011.81 =	-15% Actual ROR
1992 Cash flow, after exp.	$1,604.80
$1,604.80 ÷ $9,011.81 =	18% Actual ROR
1993 Cash flow, after exp.	-$ 283.43
(-$283.43) ÷ $9,011.81 =	-3% Actual ROR
1988-1993 Cash Flow Totals	$ 6,956.54
Mortgage Reduced (incl'd in note)	$30,171.39
Total Landlord Benefits	$37,127.93

(Project Cash Flow ÷ Amount Invested)
÷ Years Owned
= Average Annual Project Rate Of Return

($6,956.54 ÷ $9,011.81) ÷ 5.5 Yrs.
= 14% Average Annual Project ROR

When I Sold W/O Agent.

By the time I sold the row 5.5 years later the balance owed was $29,828.61 with 3.5 years remaining. My payment was high originally because of the short term, quick-payback scheme that I practice on my keeper portfolio properties.

My buyer desired cash flow to help put his son through college and subscribed to the philosophy of long term financing and increased cash flow. Myself, I was simply consolidating my properties and was tired of running down to the Southend of Columbus for collection and maintenance purposes.

We agreed upon a selling price of $82,500 with a contract down payment of $6,500. The buyer's down payment was $3,196.66 after credits and the actual amount received by me after credits and expenses was $3,452.41. (I had collected the $1,500 in rents and turned $1,250 over at closing with no real cost to me. Also, that 1500 will not count as his own, so we will add that into his input. Furthermore, since the deposits aren't really his, I will add that amount to his input.)

I agreed to carry a Land Sales Contract for $76,000 @ 8% for 20 years. His payment to me would be $635.71, whereby my payment for 3.5 more years would still be $844.75. This would be an immediate loss for me for those 42 months of $209.04, totaling 8,779.68.

My Buyer's Analysis.

Purchase Price	$82,500.00	My Buyer's PITI	$ 805.00
Land Contract	$76,000.00	Mo. Rental Income	$1,500.00
PI	$ 635.71	My Buyer's PITI	-$ 805.00
		30% Vac. & Mant.	-$ 450.00
		My Buyer's Mo. Cash Flow	**$ 245.00**

$2,940 ÷ $4,696.66 = 63% Conservative ROR

$8,340 ÷ $4,696.66 = 178% Aggressive ROR

My buyer received a better return than I did when I bought because his payment was $209.04 lower than mine. With this return and monthly cash flow, my buyer can aid himself in sending his son to college. I am sure that he did not fully understand my profit motive involved with this sale and believed that I made a serious mistake. At first glance, this begins to look quite half-witted and foolish on my part. But permit me to explain the method to my madness.

My Profit Summary.

There were 42 payments on my 1st mortgage at resale.

Conservative Outlook		Aggressive Outlook	
Down payment	-$ 9,011.81	Down payment	-$ 9,011.81
Cash flow inc.	$ 6,956.54	Cash flow inc.	$ 6,956.54
Selling credit	$ 3,452.41	Selling credit	$ 3,452.41
Deficit payments	$	Deficit pmts.	-$ 8,779.68
Note face value	$76,000.00	Note if paid out	$152,570.40
Face 1st mort.	-$29,828.61	1st if paid out	-$ 35,479.50
Net profit	**$47,568.53**	**Net profit**	**$109,708.36**

($47,568.53 ÷ $9,011.81) ÷ 5.5 Yrs

=96% Average Annual Project Consv ROR

$$(\$109{,}708.36 \div \$17{,}791.49) \div 20 \text{ Yrs}$$
$$= 31\% \text{ Aver. Ann Project Aggr ROR}$$

My selling credit of $3,452.41 helped offset this deficit series of payments of $8,779.68 over the 3.5 year period, but still left a deficit of $5,327.27. Moreover, I also have an additional amount of $9,011.81 that I used on my down payment to account for. Both of these dangling negative amounts total $14,339,08.

After my 1st mortgage of $29,828.61 is paid off in 3.5 years, the balance my buyer owes me on my Land Sales Contract will be $67,769.11, payable with the same $635.71 for a remaining 16.5 years. This money is all mine, barring income taxes. If he pays the balance off early, in 3.5 years for example, he will owe the $67,769.11. If, on the other hand, the note pays out for the entire length of the term of the remaining 16.5 years, my buyer will make 198 more payments, that I keep, totaling $125,870.58. Annually, I could receive almost $7,629 for 16.5 years.

Now, permit me to address the $17,791.49 of my own funds that I used for my down payment and deficit payments. Conservatively, my $9,011.81 was transformed into a selling credit of $3,452.41 and a note, my share, of $46,171.39 @ 8% after a 3.5 year waiting period, and $6,956.54 landlording income. My aggressive perception would be that it was turned into a series of payments and net income of $109,708.36 from 1987 to the year 2013.

My Project Analysis.

Based upon the most scrutinized method, my $9,011.81 investment was transformed into $47,568.53. Even still, is that so bad? Granted, it is not the $109,708.36 figure that is possible, but it still represents an increase of over five-fold. With a full term payout, as I predict, the amount received would be nearly six-fold.

From an overview perspective, you can examine my $70,000 purchase price and selling price of $82,500. This simple analysis demonstrates that I really only made $12,500 @ 8% on the sale. So how is it that I created a note for $46,171.39 @ 8%? (This is the difference between the note I created and the balance of my first mortgage.) The payment schedule of my buyer over the first 3.5 years, where I do suffer losses, pays off my 1st mortgage balance quicker with principle payments. Conversely, my buyer is really only paying interest on his own note.

More specifically, after 3.5 years my balance due of $29,828.61 on my 1st mortgage will be paid out and the Land Sales Contract to my buyer has reduced by only $8,230.89. Here alone, I gain an additional profit of $21,597.72!

Again my principle reduces quickly because my loan is in the final 3.5 years and my buyer's mortgage reduces slowly because he is at the beginning of a full 20 year payout. More specifically, at the point of my selling, my principle to interest ratio was greater than 2 to 1. My buyer will not reach even a level 2 to 1 ratio until June, 2007.

Selling FHA, VA, and PMM's

This example best explains the reasoning for strategy, calculation, and proper structuring of all notes. On the surface, most investors would perceive my note as simple-minded. But now you know better. Whether you perceive my net as $109,708.36, as I do, or $47,568.53 as some of you do, it does not really matter. Whichever the case, either calculation demonstrates high profit with the implementation of an abstract idea with deficit payments, thereby providing you complex note expertise which you require for increasing profits. Sometimes the smallest and subtle restructuring of your notes could enhance your profits considerably and turn that lemon into an awesome note.

Once again I did not request a balloon payment because of the potential for netting $109,708.36 over the long haul. I am always looking ahead. Moreover, at this stage I want income, not cash. If I were to insert a balloon clause on a deal like this, though, the ideal point in time would be after the 1st mortgage was paid off after 3.5 years. In that case, I would receive $67,769.11 in a lump sum payment at that time.

Furthermore, leveling the income with the installment method keeps the annual income lower, and thereby makes it easier to chip away with other deductions and tax credits. One balloon like this would be difficult to shelter from income taxes. Two would be devastating.

CHAPTER 6

LARGE CASH SUMS and LOAN-FREE APPLICATIONS

Plan III: High Rollers (FAST & SLOW FLIPS).

Whether you pay cash for your properties or you get them paid off over a period of time, the procedure for carrying notes with zero balances is the same. There are no mortgages or liens in either situation and you will carry financing with an asking down payment of less than $4,000 on smaller properties in order to attract a higher number of potential buyers. Sometimes your buyers will put more money down upon their own insistence with the goal of lower monthly payments and/or to persuade you to reduce the price.

Also, I have suggested that you remain in the smaller units for many reasons, but there remains the possibility that you have already accumulated many units that do not fall into this category. The bigger properties often require much larger down payments and a different caliber of investors. You will weigh your position and then make the necessary adjustments. In these situations, the owner financing technique itself remains intact, except huge down payments are realistic and advised.

Cash buyers do not have the same input and repair limitations of $4,000 in the smaller units as with buyers who are restricted by fewer cash dollars to invest. Although you exceed this amount with your purchase alone you will still refrain from exorbitant and unnecessary repairs and limit overall repairs to accommodate the price and repair bill total of around $20,000.

For example, if the purchase price is $14,000 you can allow yourself around $6,000 for overall costs and repairs. However, if the purchase price is $17,000 you still allow around $3,000 for the costs and repairs. The $20,000 figure is a guideline which you sometimes exceed based upon the economic and profit climate and better neighborhoods. However, most of the time my figures have fallen below or slightly above the magic number of $20,000.

Landlord cash flow is not integrated in this chapter's examples because you may utilize Plan III as a fast turnover plan. If so, properties held for 30 years with ever changing rents distort the figures and makes comparisons impossible. The landlord cash flow for the first few years was outlined in Chapter 5, so I will eliminate that perspective here. Consequently, the project net profit in all 3 examples do not reflect any landlord income.

EXAMPLE 6A

When I Bought W/Agent.

When I purchased this property initially, the building was boarded-up. The purchase price was $16,000 and repairs were an additional $5,500. My investment was approximately $21,500 cash. Also, I utilized a real estate agent to acquire the deal.

You'll notice that I exceeded the $20,000 guideline. Remember the other guideline of buying $10,000-20,000 under market? Stay close to both figures, with the latter being more important.

When I Sold W/O Agent.

Down Payment	$13,097.82	
Note of	$26,500.00	8% for 20 years
PI	$ 221.66	

$5,406 ÷ $21,500 = 25% Conservative ROR
$7,980 ÷ $21,500 = 37% Aggressive ROR

My buyer on this particular deal was a beginning investor who desired both low payments and a price reduction based upon a higher down payment. We agreed that with a down payment of $15,000 the purchase price would be lowered from $45,000 to $41,500.

She also did not know whether to have me finance for 15 or 30 years, and I offered no recommendation. She deduced that since she was unsettled on a financing strategy that the property would be carried for 20 years.

My original asking price was firm at $45,000 because of the superior building, better neighborhood, and quality Section 8 tenants with monthly rents then totaling $805. In addition, with owner financing you can ask for more on the purchase price, whereas $45,000 for this area was still low, comparatively speaking. (When I decide to sell and obtain a note, I offer the property as desirable in condition as possible to unload quickly.)

The down payment I received was $12,292.82 since I advanced her $805 for the Section 8 rents I would be receiving in a couple of days. Consequently, my selling credit was actually $13,097.82. I provided a 1st mortgage of $26,500 @ 8% for 20 years with a PI payment of $221.66 with provisions of a 10% late charge after 10 days.

My Buyer's Analysis.

1st Mtge. Note	$26,500	My Buyer's PITI	$289.23
Contract down pmt	$15,000	Mo. Rental Income	$805.00
		My Buyer's PITI	-$289.23
		30% Vac. & Maint.	-$241.50
	My Buyer's Mo. Cash Flow		**$274.27**

$3,291. ÷ $13,097.82 = 25% Conserv. ROR

$6,189.24 ÷ $13,097.82 = 47% Aggr. ROR

My Profit Summary.

Conservative Outlook		Aggressive Outlook	
Down payment	-$16,000.00	Down payment	-$16,000.00
Repairs	-$ 5,500.00	Repairs	-$ 5,500.00
Selling credit	$13,097.82	Selling credit	$13,097.82
Note face value	$26,500.00	Note if paid out	$53,198.40
Net profit	$18,097.82	Net profit	$44,796.22

Amount still invested: $21,500 - $13,097.82 = $8,402.18

$2,659.92 ÷ $8,402.18 = 32% Annual Note ROR

$$\$18,097.82 \div \$8,402.18 = 22\% \text{ Conservative}$$
$$\text{Project ROR}$$
$$(\$44,796.22 \div \$8,402.18) \div 20 \text{ Years}$$
$$= 27\% \text{ Aggressive Project ROR}$$

My net profit ranges right now from $18,097.82 to $44,796.22 depending upon your perspective. Only when the loan is ultimately paid off will the true figures unfold. Right now, though, the annual note income is $2,659.92.

My Project Summary.

The cash down payment and repairs totaling approximately $21,500 were heavily reduced with the $13,097.82 that I recovered at closing. This leaves my input at $8,402.18.

The benefit from this investment is that during my ownership I received a landlord cash flow and after selling I acquired a mortgage note for $26,500 payable @ 8% for 20 years @ $221.66 per month totaling $53,198.40 in income payments if all payments are made. My perception is that I turned $8,402.18 cash into monthly income ranging from $18,097.82 to $53,198.40.

EXAMPLE 6B

When I Bought W/Agent.

This double cost me $19,608.18 at closing. One side had just been totally redone with insurance money due to water damage from tenant destruction and the other was in good shape. Renters from Section 8 were soon installed after closing with the rents at $395 per side.

Purchase Price	$19,608.18
Rents	$ 790.00

$6,036 ÷ $19,608.18 = 31% Conservative ROR
$8,880 ÷ $19,608.18 = 45% Aggressive ROR

When I Sold W/Agent.

Selling Price	$29,500.00		
Down Payment	$20,172.50		
$8,000 note	**$ 400.00**	**interest**	**two 3-month pmts.**

Sometimes you encounter cash buyers who fall short on the entire purchase price. You can simply accommodate them by selling with a note for that smaller amount or by installing mortgage notes with a series of short term balloon payments.

This double was sold for $29,500. My buyer put $20,172.50 down and I secured the balance of $8,000 with a 1st mortgage and note payable with 2 payments of $4,000 each with $400 in interest. I permitted him to specify his own payment schedule, it turned out to be the following April and July, because only he knew his financial status and I wanted a good quality note. At the closing I received $17,755.50.

This was a bit uncommon, but a real estate agent who I knew for many years proposed the offer. (You'll make note that I utilized an agent for selling.) In most cases, it would be a straight cash deal and would not be entered into this book. However, my example does involve a note and should be considered as a viable alternative if your buyer states that he is beyond his cash limit.

My Buyer's Analysis.

The rents at the time of sale were $365 per side.

$6,132 ÷ $28,572.50 = 21% Conservative ROR
$8,160 ÷ $28,572.50 = 29% Aggressive ROR

My Profit Summary.

Down payment	-$19,608.18
Selling credit	$17,755.50
Balloon Note	$ 8,400.00
Net profit	$ 6,547.32

26155.50 ÷ $19,608.18 = 133% Project ROR

As you're beginning to realize, my investments do not always make enormous amounts of money, nor do I expect them to. My rate of return was 133%, yet my profit was only $6,547.32 cash. Would I make this investment again? Yes, any day of the week, every week.

EXAMPLE 6C

When I Bought W/Agent.

This double was already rented and in decent condition when I bought it. I raised the $300 rent and $300 deposit on each side to $350 when vacancies arose. I purchased this double through a real estate agent and paid $19,264.74 cash at closing. The cash flow reflects $50 monthly additional for taxes and insurance.

$$\$5,280 \div \$19,264.74 = 27\% \text{ Conservative ROR}$$
$$\$7,800 \div \$19,264.74 = 40\% \text{ Aggressive ROR}$$

When I Sold W/O Agent.

Sales Price	$35,000.00		
Down Pmt.	$ 5,000.00		
Selling Credit	$ 3,126.72		
$30,000 note		@ 8% for 15 years	=286.70 monthly

The contract sales price was $35,000 accompanied with a $5,000 down payment. At the closing my buyer brought $3,618.39. After subtracting my selling credit of $3,126.72 my remaining cash investment was $16,138.02. In essence, I exchanged this cash for a $30,000 note @ 8% payable for 15 years @ 286.70 per month. This is nearly twice my cash investment. Also, the bank's savings interest rates at that time were slightly over 3%.

My Buyer's Analysis.

Mtge. note	$30,000	Mo. Pmt.	$ 286.70
Down pmt.	$ 5,000	Est. Taxes And Ins.	$ 50.00
		Cash at closing	$ 3,618.39
		My Buyer's PITI	$ 336.70
		Mo. Rental Income	$ 700.00
		My Buyer's PITI	-$ 336.70
		30% Vac. & Maint.	-$ 210.00
		My Buyer's Mo. Cash Flow	**$ 153.30**

$1,839.60 ÷ $3,618.39 = 51% Conserv. ROR
$4,359.60 ÷ $3,618.39 = 120% Aggr. ROR

My Profit Summary.

Conservative Outlook		Aggressive Outlook	
Down payment	-$19,264.74	Down payment	-$19,264.74
Selling credit	$ 3,126.72	Selling credit	$ 3,126.72
Note face value	$30,000.00	Note if paid out	$51,606.00
Net profit	$13,861.98	Net profit	$35,467.98

$3,440.40 ÷ $16,138.02 = 21% Annual Note
ROR
$13,861.98 ÷ $16,138.02 = 86% Conservative
Project ROR
($35,467.98 ÷ $16,138.02) ÷ 15 Yrs.
= 15% Aggressive ROR

If the all the payments are made for the entire 15 years I will receive a total of $51,606. My note face value of $30,000 is $13,861.98 above my actual cash input and I also get nearly 5% above the bank rate. Some entrepreneurs who lend money to investors who want simply to obtain a higher interest rate than the current 3%. They may settle for just the additional 5% on my investment of $16,138.02. Moreover, I not only get the additional interest rate on the principle balance, but an increase on the principle balance plus 8% on that balance as well.

CHAPTER 7

OPTION TO PURCHASE

Plan IV: Unique And Obscure (FAST-FLIP).

This technique encompasses only advantages of virtually no risk of liability or cash investment. The brilliance of this plan is that you will never actually own property, rather control it. You will profit from the resale just like an owner would. In essence, you can sell a property like an owner could, but you do not have the deed in your name, nor have any of the ownership liabilities and responsibilities. In other words, you are not liable for any mortgages due on the property, do not collect rent, or make repairs. You will not make any repairs whatsoever with this technique because you are neither an owner, nor a landlord. What you are, however, is a contract buyer that has the power to back out of the deal, purchase the property yourself, or assign your option to another buyer with an added profit for yourself. This profit can be in the form of cash or a note. Primarily, a note will be obtained to quicken the sale. You will utilize the same philosophy as in the other plans: the lower the cash down payment, the faster the sale.

Don't confuse this technique with Lease With The Option To Purchase. That is an entirely different method discussed in Chapters 8, 10, and 12.

Contract Down Payment.

Contracts to buy with this plan will only be written as an Option To Purchase, which entitles you to back out anytime without recourse. Earnest money will be $1 to $100. Your liability will be limited only by the earnest money deposit and advertising costs because you will not take deeds to any properties. Preferably, your offers will involve a $1 earnest money deposit. In Ohio, real estate purchase and option contracts require at least a $1 cash deposit to be valid and enforceable. A $1 deposit with the contract works primarily on acquaintances, referrals, and contacts who have confidence that you can swiftly unload their properties for them. In the event that the option is fulfilled, the $100 deposit, for example, is returned to you.

No Sales Commissions.

This plan suggests that no real estate agent will be used upon resale. Since you never really buy real estate with this plan you needn't enlist the aid of agents for option contracts. Ordinarily, you would need a license from your state to sell property for others. However, since you have an option to buy, you have an interest in ownership. Owners are permitted to sell their own properties without licenses. (However, in some states, this does not include optionees advertising to sell in the newspaper.) You simply advertise, (state laws permitting), call your contacts, and sell by the same methods previously discussed in the earlier chapters.

Realistically, the sales commission ordinarily paid to agents is much of your profit.

When Ideal To Implement.

These deals in small numbers are not profitable enough to fully sustain a decent lifestyle, nor are they recommended to occupy your entire work week. They are, however, designed to provide an additional outlet for when you locate properties that you personally do not want to own, yet an anxious seller is providing good terms. Rather than giving the deal to a friend and not financially benefiting from this find yourself, you can implement this method and turn a quick profit.

You might ask, "If it is such a good deal, why don't you buy it yourself?"

That would be a good question. Personally, I have consolidated all of my inner-city portfolio properties into one location making rent collection and repairs a breeze. In fact, all of the wasted time that I was spending on the road traveling from one property to another property is now spent totally away from all currently owned properties and being spent in more productive ways. For this reason alone, I personally might not be interested in putting a particular deed in my name.

Other investors might find that three pages of code violations with a vindictive and relentless city inspector to be a bit much to endure. Furthermore, if a property is in dire need of repair, the total cost of restoration may exceed many investors' budgets.

Finally, sometimes the margin of profit to flip the deal is too small to justify all the trouble and liability associated in the first 3 plans. If your margin for profit is only $2,000, why exert energy and expenses on a closing to buy and a closing to sell? Wouldn't it make more sense to just have one closing and have the seller incur all of the expenses? Absolutely. All you will do is find a willing seller, a good buyer, and take a cut for yourself. That cut will vary on the agreement you have with the seller and the amount of equity involved.

Locating And Negotiating With These Sellers: A Breed Apart.

These sellers are not the easiest to locate, nor are they the hardest either. I find that the best way to find these sellers is to stumble onto them while searching for properties for myself to buy. Since I am virtually always looking for deals through the newspaper and am in constant contact with other real estate agents and investors, I manage to encounter this opportunity without even trying. The only criterion is to find sellers who have assumable properties not listed with agents and are willing to give you a chance to sell it. Rather than be unscrupulous and acting like you personally are really going to close the deal, divulge your plan to actively unload the property for him and get a profit for yourself. Simply find the lowest amount that the seller will take with the smallest down payment and then spring you proposal on him.

You can start negotiating by taking all above his selling price and conclude with a 50/50 split all above his original selling price. Now, this deal will hopefully appeal to his innate sense of greed. He will envision getting 50% of your efforts without costing him a thing. Insure that the seller pays all the usual closing costs at no expense to you. This honesty can assist in contracting the deal and not giving but a $1 deposit. If you need to say one more thing to close the deal, state that rather than your preferred 90-day contract expiration, you will option for 60, 45, or 30 days. (Shorter periods are fine as a last resort and even all right if $100 is given.) Conclude by stating that you will advertise in the Sunday paper until you sell the property or the contract expires and that you and he together will conduct the showings, when possible. This way, if your showing goes well, you can write the sale immediately. Your buyers will put down a $500 earnest money deposit on each property with you, with no weasel clauses. If the deal does not close, the $500 is yours providing your option contract so states.

Market Conditions.

Insofar as your profit is concerned, you need to have a feel for market prices and adequately gauge the equity after paying the seller. If you have a real knowledge for the current market conditions, you will know immediately what is possible to resell for and also whether or not your seller has allowed enough equity for you to expend your time and advertising money.

In my city, I know that just about any double in run-down condition will sell for $30,000 when habitable, and $40,000 if very little work is needed. However, this is only the case if the loans are assumable, the units are rented, and the down payments are less than $4,000. As the market changes from season to season, I know that sometimes investors will pay $35,000 or $45,000 given the market conditions, or season, for the same properties. It will be up to you to figure and decide what the timing dictates, and back the figures into what the seller wants. If necessary, you can try to persuade the seller to reduce his demands to accommodate your meager profit. On the other hand, it is very possible to maintain your seller's original selling price and acquire an even larger note than I recommend.

The Contracts.

A. *Standard Real Estate Purchase Contract:*
   To Buy.

You can structure your contract with a standard real estate contract obtained from your local Board Of Realtors with a closing to take place in 45 to 90 days and insert weasel clauses like property inspections, attorney's approval, contingent upon another deal closing, etc. This method assures full refund of earnest money deposit. Insure that after your signature you put a comma and "his (or her) successors and assigns." This legally allows you to assign your contract to another investor.

One problem with this contract is that most sellers are impatient and they want you to sign off contingencies within a couple of days. However, if you have explained your full intentions to the seller that you do not intend to own the property yourself, this will not be a problem. You can install one weasel clause without ever signing off on it or being hounded to do so, not to mention that showings would be difficult. In essence, these examples fully illustrate the necessity to keep everything above board.

B. *Option To Purchase Contract: To Buy.*

This is the more practical agreement to enter into. You can specify your full intentions, and insert or delete sections of the contract when necessary. With this type of agreement, you should be able to dissuade the seller from accepting a large deposit from you. The seller and your buyer will conduct business as they ordinarily would have, only you take a note from the closing.

If you must, put $50 to $100 down in consideration of the right and option to purchase. Naturally, you will require from your buyer that amount which you gave to seller. In all practicality, at least $500 down from your buyer is best.

You can hire an attorney to formulate your own basic option to purchase contract. From that contract forward, you can delete provisions that do not apply and insert any additions that you require. You can, however, obtain a generic contract if you can find one that does not encompass too much non-applicable information.

At the end of this chapter, you will find an Option To Purchase Contract that can be utilized in Ohio. Your state may be different. You can make modifications, or use it as is. Like a standard purchase contract, money is required on this particular agreement. One dollar makes it legal.

C. *Standard Real Estate Purchase Contract:*
   To Sell.

Obtain a standard real estate contract from your local Board Of Realtors and have both yourself and your seller sign in addition to your buyer. This demonstrates that both of you agree and approve of the terms set forth for your buyer.

Your buyer should put down at least $500 down earnest money deposit on each property he writes into contract. One way to combat your seller's closing expenses, providing he does not want any money, is to specify that your buyer puts a total down payment of $1,000, $500 down and $500 at the closing. This usually offsets all of the seller's expenses. Bring the $500 to the closing and apply it to the seller's expenses. The major goal will be to insure that the seller not bring money to the closing. Any money you need to leave the closing with will be you own earnest money deposit and possibly your advertising fees. On occasion, if the opportunity exists, you can leave the closing with a sum of money. However, I am just focusing upon what you try to minimally receive at the closing. (You can make changes as situations arise.)

Your closing will be set for 30 days. Title insurance can be provided by most companies in 2-3 days for cash deals, but you must wait for the loan assumption packet to arrive. Do not include any weasel clauses for your buyer. Don't permit anyone to tie up the property. If an investor wants a partner to see it, delay the showing until both are present. If you find out about the partner after the showing, then postpone the contract until the other partner inspects the property. Work out any and all contingencies before writing the contract. Remember, if the deal does not close under these circumstances, the $500 is yours. If the deal closes, the $500 goes to the seller's expenses.

EXAMPLE 7A

An investor who had previously assumed a first mortgage from me indicated that he desired to get out of the residential rental business and into the commercial aspect of real estate. He admitted that he paid too much for his properties and was too easy on his tenants. He explained that he was not making much in the way of cash flow. For him, code enforcement inspectors trying to jail him was the last straw. He asked if I wanted my double back and another one on the next street as well. I declined on the basis that I had anticipated consolidating my properties for years and I had recently accomplished that feat. He persisted by stating that he just wanted to unload the two doubles immediately. He asked if I could recommend anyone who would like to buy the properties. I immediately seized the opportunity to spring my Option To Purchase solution on him.

Since he was a friend, I structured the deal so that he and I would enter into a 50-50 equity split. He just wanted to sell out and did not expect anything further, so he jumped at my offer. We met the next day and wrote it up.

Ordinarily, I would have taken all the profits for myself, as I advise you to do so. However, for those fellow investors who you desire to maintain and continue strong lengthy business relationships, I strongly recommend an accommodating approach for its continuing success. Although my friend was willing and eager to sign over all of his equity, he would have certainly left the closing with a bad taste in his mouth, especially after seeing how much money I had made with such little effort.

My Seller's Analysis Before Sale.
Double A

1st Mtge.	$26,278.45	1st Mtge. PITI	$351.00
My Existing Note	$ 8,111.42	My Existing Note	$ 72.82
Total	$34,389.87		$423.82
		Mo. Rental Inc	$730.00
		My Seller's PITI	-$423.82
		30% Vac. & Mant.	-$ 210.00
		Mo. Cash Flow	$ 96.18

Double B

1st Mtge.	$22,559.30	1st Mtge. PITI	$366.89
		Mo. Rental Income	$600.00
		My Seller's PITI	-$366.89
		30% Vac. & Maint.	-$180.00
		Mo. Cash Flow	**$ 53.11**

There was not much to work with here because there was not much cash flow. However, doubles in the area sold from $10,000 to $50,000. I surmised that since this property was in very good condition and most investors don't calculate with a vacancy and maintenance allowance, I could sell the property for $40,000 with a down payment of $1,000. Although this was not a confident assessment, it was one that I was willing to attempt.

My existing note from when I sold to him had a balloon due in 4 1/4 years, but I readily assessed that I would be eliminating this for an increased note amount.

Although Double B had a lower cash flow, I was relying on not only the improbability of the 30% calculation being used, but the fact that I could sell this double for only $30,000 with $1,000 down. There had been three pages of city code violations, which included an exterior paint job. All had been completed, except for the gutters. The seller indicated that he had already contracted for the gutters to be hung and to inform any buyer of this fact.

These two doubles are not the textbook examples to best illustrate this technique. The ideal situation is one where the cash flow is quite high that even allows for you to leave the closing with a couple thousand dollars and a note. Just about anyone could and would take on such an easily identifiable project. Since you fully understand how the system works, I need to demonstrate to you that even less desirable situations warrant a second look. In fact, if I can make these two marginal doubles yield a return, you can imagine the magnitude of properties that could fit this mold.

The underlying secret in the potential success of these two doubles was my advertisement reading that two assumable doubles were available for $1,000 down on each. How many ads have you seen state this? Not many. That was what made these two unlikely doubles click. For would-be investors without much money, who wished to break into the market, perceived this as an ideal starting point.

Four other reasons contributed to the sale. Although the cash flow was limited, the buyers had in mind to raise rents to $350 per side, and hoped to rent to Section 8 for an even greater profit. Furthermore, I stated that the notes we would carry could be financed for whatever time frame they desired. I suggested 30 years to keep the total payments lower. Furthermore, there was a balloon due on my existing note on Double A and some people find that difficult to assume. I traded that balloon for a 30 year payout. Lastly, I reminded them of streamlining, of which they already had knowledge.

When I Sold W/O Agent.

Selling Prices	$30,000.00	$40,000.00	
Down Pmt.	$ 1,000.00	$ 1,000.00	
Note to seller for	$ 5,525.42	8% @ $ 40.56	for 30 years
My note inc. monthly from	$ 8,111.42	@ $ 72.83	W/7 year balloon due in 4.5 years
To	$13,636.83	10% @ $119.67	for 30 years W/No balloon

I did contract each double for my asking prices of $30,000 and $40,000 with $1,000 down on each to the same buyers. The seller and myself also signed the contract.

Rather than both the seller and myself co-owning a note on Double A and co-owning on another note on Double B, we figured that it would be easier for me to enlarge my existing note from Double A to be inclusive of the profits from both doubles and to provide the seller with his own note on Double B to be inclusive of both his portions as well. This modification would eliminate the hassle of receiving, signing, and dividing the monthly checks for the next 30 years on such small amounts.

The seller obtained a note for $5,525.42 @ 8% for 30 years with a monthly payment of $40.56. Over the life of the loan, if it fully pays out, my seller will receive $14,601.60. This is not bad considering that if I had bought them, he would have done much worse because I would not have put $2,000 down and would have just assumed his balances.

My Buyer's Analysis.

Purchase Price	$70,000.00	Total PITI	$ 878.12
Down Pmt.	$ 2,000.00	Total Mo. Income	$1330.00
		Total PITI	-$ 878.12
		30% Vac. & Maint.	-$ 399.00
	My Buyer's Mo. Cash Flow		**$ 52.88**

$$\$634.56 \div \$1,051.18 = 60\% \text{ Conservative ROR}$$
$$\$5,422.56 \div \$1,051.18 = 516\% \text{ Aggr. ROR}$$

It is hard to believe that such a small cash flow could yield such a high return, but the down payments being low was the reason for such high percentages. The credits at the closing kept the amount invested near the one thousand level. After the buyers raise rents, the rate of return will increase significantly.

My Profit Summary.

My original note was $8,300 @ 10% amortized for 30 years with a monthly payment of $72.83 with a 7 year balloon, payable in 4 1/4 years from that time. (51 payments.) After 33 payments reducing the mortgage balance to $8,111.42, we struck this new deal for the new buyers. As you recall, I took the profits from both doubles and put them on Double A.

Under the new agreement, my note was increased to $13,636.83 with monthly payments of $119.67 @ 10% for 30 years with no balloon. The face value of my note was increased by $5,525.41 and the monthly income was increased by $46.84 with just one advertisement costing $10.70.

$562.08 ÷ $10.70 = 5,253% Conservative ROR
$5,525.41 ÷ $10.70 = 51,639% Consv. Proj. ROR
($16,862.40 ÷ $10.70) ÷ 30 = 5,253% Aggr. Project ROR

My Project Analysis.

Your biggest objection will most assuredly be the fact that now I no longer have a balloon payment. This would be a valid criticism if the balloon payment was needed or desired by the holder. However, I am of the position and ability to overlook the necessity and desire for the payment in favor of the larger and more lengthier note. Income is my forte.

One ad was placed and I will receive an additional $5,525.41. There was one showing time that the seller and I both attended. The showing was with three different parties, two sets of partners and a single investor. It was easier to show to three different parties at the same time and sell to whoever wanted either or both doubles. The single investor was told of the credit check and he didn't even enter the units. One set of partners later met us on a luncheon date, but got cold feet when I reiterated my need for a contingency clause based upon their credit check.

The second set of partners said that they would decide and call back, which they did. We set up a dinner meeting and wrote up the deal and everyone signed. After 20 days we held the closing. The brief delay was due to all parties being available at a convenient time.

In summation, after a couple of appointments and a closing, and a $10.70 expense, the note was earned.

Features:
* *I made no repairs: the landlord made them.*
* *I collected no rents: the landlord collected them.*
* *I avoided city inspectors: the landlord completed he code list.*
* *I had no liability: the owner was on the deeds.*
* *I had no expenses: except an ad for $10.70.*
* *I made half of the profit: which is ridiculous.*

Consider the earnings if the seller was not a long term friend. My note would have been $11,050.82! Surprisingly, this deal first appeared, even to me, to be one to overlook. I am glad that I looked closer.

Investors state, "He was a long time investor and real estate agent. Why didn't he just do that himself?"

My reply is that he wanted to sell his properties immediately, was frustrated, and was familiar with the typical long term listing process. He really did not know the procedure to execute this technique anyhow. Creative financing to most investors and real estate agents is confusing and complicated because they never took the time to learn the ins and outs.

Contemplate your earnings based upon more reasonable and more opportune circum-stances. You could extend your property selection to singles, condos, or whatever with this technique. You can stray from the property type, because you have virtually nothing to lose and everything to gain. If you stray from the fundamentals, however, you subject yourself to great personal risk and liability.

My Converted Seller: Learning from the master.

Not so amazing was my friend's own inspiration and enthusiasm of what I was able to do with his properties. Not three weeks later, he called to boast about how he had located 19 assumable condos with nothing down for $25,000 each. He said that he already had a buyer, without even advertising, for $29,000 each with an entire down payment on all 19 of $3,000 with a 4 year balloon. During this 4 year period he and a partner will net a monthly profit of $700 per month. His greatest joy was explaining to me how there will be no tenants, repairs, expenses, or city inspectors to contend with, which had made him so miserable before.
He just about had the hang of it with two exceptions. One, he will be taking deeds to the properties, which he could have avoided if he had utilized the option plan. Since he chose to implement Plan I, he should have done so without owing on a 5-year balloon payment himself. I abhor owing on balloons. His response to my reservations was that he found a partner who was well to do and they are not concerned with a default dilemma on their buyer's part. (In a default situation, they would need to seek financing for their balloon on their second

mortgage.) My friend learned what to do, but not how to do it. His deal could have been perfect, without risk with just a little adjustment.

During that same conversation, he also informed me that he took my advice and tried to sell other properties to our buyers after the closing, which he did. He sold another double and a 4-unit double-duplex to the same buyers. Both of these properties were sold on Land Sales Contracts. Consequently, if his buyers default, he will not suffer the agony of a more lengthy foreclosure, as with deed transfers. Although he had overpaid originally, he actually sold the buildings for more than he paid and will experience cash flow without the landlording. He agreed that his low down payments and owner financing attracted the buyers.

OPTION TO PURCHASE CONTRACT

Notice that number 5 on the upcoming contract regarding existing encumbrances has two disclosures as examples. Regarding the Low Income Housing Tax Credits, they should be disclosed here when applicable and in your inspection/disclosure checklist. When knowing, you should also specify in the contract the Board of Realtors contract also. Secondly, there is a disclosure regarding an assessment of $45. This is an arbitrary number based upon a possible element that must be disclosed. This one relates to a sanitary sewer assessment with the remaining balance documented. The function of number five is to disclose and document disclosure of such items.

Focus your attention at the end where the OPTIONEE signs. After your signature you put a comma and write "his successors and assigns" as was explained earlier.

Option To Purchase Real Estate

This Agreement dated _____January 1_____, ____1997___, by and between
_____Seller_____ and _____Seller's Spouse_____
(hereinafter referred to as "Landowners"), and _____Investor_____
(hereinafter referred to as "Optionee").

For And In Consideration of the sum of _____One Dollar ($1.00)_____
paid by the Optionee to the Landowners, the receipt whereof is hereby acknowledged, the Landowners hereby sell and grant unto said Optionee, his heirs and assigns, the right and option to purchase the following described real estate, in which the Landowners hold title as an estate in fee simple absolute, together with inchoate right of dower, for the total purchase price of _____Twenty-Thousand_____
_____Dollars ($20,000)_____.

Situated in the _____City of Tremont_____, County of _____Pleasant_____
State of _____Ohio_____.

Being Lot ___123___ in the _____Many Trees_____ Subdivision as the same is numbered and delineated upon the recorded plat thereof of record in Plat Book ___7___, page ___75___, Recorder's office, _____Pleasant_____ County, _____Ohio_____.

Further, upon the consideration and grants above set forth, the parties agree:

1. **Extent of Option:** This right and option shall extend to, and be effective until ___March 31___, ___1997___, at midnight.

2. **Exercise of Option:** Said right and option to purchase may be exercised by the giving of notice to the Landowners by notification of the closing itself by the closing agent before such time of expiration of the right of option. The deposit will be refunded at closing.

3. **Failure to Exercise Option:** Upon the failure of the Optionee to exercise said right and option in the manner described in this Agreement, said sum of ___One Dollar___ ___($1.00)___, i.e., consideration, shall be the sole property of the Landowners, without further obligation on his part under this Agreement.

4. **Terms of Purchase:** The purchase price shall be the assumable loan balance of approximately ___Eighteen Thousand Five Hundred___ ___($18,500___), plus a down payment of approximately ___Fifteen Hundred Dollars___ ___($1,500___), said sum to total ___$20,000___ Seller will provide title insurance, pay closing fees, pro-rate taxes, rents, turn over rental deposits up to and at closing. Seller to maintain property, owner, and landlord responsibilities up to closing, and make showings possible for buyer's clients; continue payments and rent collection, etc. Deed shall be transferred at closing. Landowners represent that their mortgage is assumable by any Optionee. In the event the subject mortgage cannot be assumed, the Optionee shall be entitled to a refund of his deposit and this option agreement shall be void and of no force and effect.

5. **Existing Encumbrances:** There will be no clouds on title at closing. If they appear, Optionee to give Landowner 15 days extension to clear them.

   Exceptions: <u>There is a balance of 8 years in Low Income Housing</u> <u>Tax Credits. There is an assessment of $45 for a balance 16</u> <u>months.</u>

6. **Closing:** Closing to take place within the deadline of option. Upon notification of excise of option by the closing agent, seller to promptly provide appropriate information and documentation for a speedy sale. Optionee shall not be in breach of this agreement if Optionee has a buyer and said buyer fails to perform in his contract to buy with Optionee. If so, Optionee continues option and may again assert his option to buy anytime before the expiration date.

7. **Alienability of Rights:** This Agreement shall be binding upon the next of kin, devisees, executors, administrators, guardians, other personal representatives, successors, and assigns of the parties hereto. The rights and options created under this Agreement may be assigned, devised, bequeathed, 54 extended. However, any modification of any portion of this agreement must be made in writing and signed by all parties.

9. **Gender:** All words in this agreement, including the words Landowners and Optionee, shall be construed to include the plural as well and the singular number, words used herein in the present tense shall include the future as well as the present, and words used in the masculine gender shall include the feminine and neuter.

Executed and acknowledged
in the presence of:

_____
Bank Teller

_____
Bank Loan Officer

_____
Seller
Landowner

_____
Seller's Spouse
Landowner

_____
Investor, his successors & assigns
Optionee

CHAPTER 8

LEASE WITH THE OPTION
TO PURCHASE

Plan V: Concurrent Flipping And Landlording (Fast-Flip).

This gives investors like myself who enjoy both a Fast-Flip and a continual interest in properties. In essence, you sell a house and distance yourself from it, yet you maintain an ownership interest.

This plan focuses on cheaper single homes in depressed areas. You can increase the price range given your area and expertise. However, I find that investing in depressed areas facilitates my lower risk and higher profit theories. Therefore, this plan is geared to that price range.

Your will not take exception to the assumability clauses regarding loans and financing. You will not be selling for cash and paying off the loan. It will be ultimately wrapped on Land Sales Contract, but it will not risk the calling of the note.

After securing a deed with financing by way of FHA, VA, and PMM's, your attention will be directed toward getting the unit ready for resale and installing a tenant/buyer. I've found the consensus among investors is to immediately give a Land Sales Contract to owner-occupants with a single down payment of $2,000-4,000. To these, I strongly disagree. It is too soon to enter into a Land Sales Contract with those with marginal income and credit, and the one-time down payment is often too high for these buyers.

Stalling The Process.

Many investors who immediately sell by Land Sales Contract find themselves in the courthouse trying to regain their properties from buyers who have defaulted. Most of those who I've spoken with have stated that they did not run credit checks.

It is a little more involved than simply evicting someone. Rather than a 3-day notice, a 30-day notice must be given. However, if a lawyer intervenes, it could possibly take even longer. (Your area may be different.) Wouldn't it make more sense to have a 3 year trial run, if it were possible? Even if you had rented to that buyer before for many years, wouldn't you agree that a Land Sales Contract is more involved than just a lease and more would be expected from the tenant/buyer? If it were feasible to structure a situation where you could have a trial run before entering into a Land Sales Contract, wouldn't you do so before getting entangled into such a contract? This is where the **Lease With The Option To Purchase** comes in.

You Lease-Option for 3 years. This will be your trial run. If your payment is $300, your buyer's Lease-Option will be $450 to $500. Out of the rent, $50 monthly will accrue during the trial period. During the three year period, your tenant could accumulate $1800 towards the purchase price.

Down Payments.

Find a single home where your input, down payment and repairs, is $4,000 or less, just like the other plans. The less you have invested in the project, the less cash down you can charge your buyer.

The Lease-Option could require $1,100 down upon moving in, and another $1,100 upon exercising the option. Couple this $2,200 with the $1,800 equity build-up and you have $4,000. Isn't this much easier for these buyers to obtain than by advertising a down payment of $4,000? Remember, if you only have $2,000 in the property, you can have a $1,000 payment at each end, or even $500 at each end, depending upon the intensity or urgency of the situation. The equity build-up will take care of, and even exceed, the balance of your cash input.

Finding Buyers.

Another objective is to find a select tenant who would like to rent to own. For investors who have a pool of tenants, they are easy to find. In fact, you can scan your tenant list and easily identify those who are long term tenants, pay promptly, and are virtually no trouble.

Furthermore, I contend that this is better than a credit check. Am I suggesting that you could sell to a tenant without a credit check? No. But I am suggesting that some leniency may be in order. On the one hand, it is a tough neighborhood. Furthermore, if you have rented to someone who has paid timely for many years, interacted with you with respect and consideration, and you have compiled no complaints, you have a good chance of continuing your good fortune. Of course, a credit check on anyone is no guarantee of receiving money. It is my contention that I would rather sell to someone with whom I have successfully dealt with in the past. Plus, it expedites finding a buyer. Simply, ask select tenants if they would like to rent with the option to buy. Otherwise, run an advertisement in the newspaper.

Who Makes Repairs?

Insure that there is a good roof and working mechanics. These items may be too expensive for most tenants. It would be wisest to have all cosmetics completed. You can stray from this based upon your buyer's capabilities, but I wouldn't advise it. It would not be worth sacrificing the purchase price.

Insofar as repairs are concerned, the Lease-Option will state that all repairs be shifted to the buyer. You can make arrangements for your buyer to pay you for work on the property, or provide phone numbers of cheap workers.

Furthermore, your option contract should state that if the property is subsequently shackled with city code violations, the tenant/buyer is responsible for them. If the seller makes the repairs because the tenant is uncooperative or doesn't have the immediate funds, the seller will bill the tenant/buyer, and he must repay within 30 days or the Lease-Option is terminated. If the latter prevails, the option fee and $50 option payments belong to you. It would be time now to find a new buyer. Wouldn't you be glad that you weren't stuck with a Land Sales Contract in this situation?

What Are The Terms?

For this particular deal, I recommend a $20,000 price above your own purchase price. During the Lease-Option period, insure a net of $150-$200 monthly. Upon the Land Sales Contract, $150 monthly net will suffice. (Taxes and insurance will be the responsibility of the buyer after the L.S.C. has been signed.)

The interest rate that you charge really shouldn't vary that much. You want to charge the maximum allowable from one individual to another. If you are doing business as a corporation, I would still recommend remaining in the individual maximum range. (For your general information, when I last checked there was no limit for corporations charging corporations.) Be apprised to find out the current legal interest fee limits as suggested in Chapter 1.

Construct the loan term at your own discretion. Just insure that the time frame is at least as long as your loan. I recommend 30 years. To insure a more affordable payment for your buyer, and more income during your lifetime.

In essence, your Land Sales Contract will be a wrap. Your 8 year loan @ 8% interest would flourish on a 30 year loan @ 12% for $20,000 more than what you paid.

What Happens After 3 Years?

Within the 3 year period, your buyer may exercise his option anytime by way of a bank loan. Your contract can specify that this is what will transpire. After a legitimate loan rejection in 3 years, you can enter into a Land Sales Contract, grant an extension to the Lease-Option, or remove the buyer and start again.

My recommendation is to follow through with the Fast-Flip. Provide an arena for success. Hold out the golden carrot, *home-ownership*. Create a viable opportunity for a renter to become a homeowner, even after a financial institutional rejection. Let them know that if they pay on time for 3 years, not bother you with repairs, and make that final down payment, you will grant them a Land Sales Contract. They must feel that the home will definitely be theirs, even after a bank rejection. Granting to them that fact in writing should enhance their performance.

Bank Financing: Surely, you jest!

Hopefully, 5% of these buyers will find financing. You could increase the odds by helping to directing fruitless buyers toward a **mortgage broker**. These brokers help find financing for the hard to approve buyers. It doesn't always work, but it is worth a try.

Summary.

For investors who keep a portfolio of properties, notes, and engage in Fast-Flip tactics, this is ideal. You can flip houses. Upon default, it works out better than the usual landlording. The rents and deposits (option fees) are higher and the repairs are gone. Upon default, you have larger deposits and rents to keep. Within 3 years, it is a simple eviction. If things work out as intended, though, you've covered all the bases and made some money. This is the conservative outlook for which I am so noted.

Lease is compliments of FABCO,
4640 Executive Dr., Columbus, Ohio 43220

Notice on the upcoming lease:
    Term - three years.
    Security Deposit - zero.

Rental Agreement

READ CAREFULLY, THIS IS A LEGAL AND BINDING CONTRACT

This Rental Agreement, made this _____ day of _____, 19 _____, by and between _____

_____ the owner of the premises, described below, said owner being here-

inafter referred to as "Owner," through its agent _____,

hereinafter referred to as "Agent," and _____.

hereinafter referred to as "Resident."

WITNESSETH, that Owner, in consideration of the rent to be paid and the covenants and agreements to be performed by Resident, does hereby

rent the following described premises, to wit: Situated in the City of _____

County of _____ and State of _____,

known as _____.

TERM AND PAYMENTS

Resident agrees to occupy said premises for an Original term of _____ **3 years** ,

said term to commence on the _____, 19 _____, and agrees to pay without demand the rental of $ _____

payable on equal monthly installments of $ _____ on or before the 1st of each and every month beginning on

_____ 1st, 19 _____. Any and all payments to be paid by the Resident under this agreement are to be

paid to _____,

at _____.

or such other place as shall be designated by _____

All payments are to be made in cash, certified check, or money orders or other method approved by the Owner or Agent.

ADDITIONAL RENT FOR LATE PAYMENT

In the event Resident pays any monthly installment after the **2ND** day of the month, additional rent of $ _____

per day for late payment with a maximum charge of _____.

1. **ACCELERATION.** If Resident fails to pay any installment of rent when same becomes due and payable, the entire amount due under this agreement shall at once become due and payable.

2. **SECURITY DEPOSIT.** Resident has deposited with the Owner or Agent a Security Deposit in the amount of $ _ZERO_ . Said Security Deposit is to guarantee the return of the premises to the Owner in the same or better condition as when accepted by the Resident, reasonable wear excepted. The Security Deposit is to indemnify Owner against damage and/or loss of value as a result of Resident's action, mistake, or inaction during the term of occupancy. The Security Deposit may not be applied by the Resident as and for payment of any rent due the Owner prior to the vacation of the premises by the Resident. Should the Resident be responsible for damage and/or loss of value to the premises greater than the value of the Security Deposit, Resident agrees to reimburse the Owner for such loss immediately upon presentation of a bill for said damage and/or loss.

3. **NOTICE TO TERMINATE AND RENEWAL.** Unless another rental agreement is signed by the parties hereto or unless written notice of termination is given by one party to the other thirty (30) days before expiration of this agreement, this contract shall be automatically renewed on a month-to-month basis and may be terminated thereafter by either party upon the giving of written notice to the other party thirty (30) days prior to the next periodic rental due date. Resident shall include with said notice a forwarding address if one is available. Termination shall take place only on the last day of any given month unless otherwise agreed to in writing.

Upon vacating Resident agrees to return the premises to the Owner in the same or better condition as when received, reasonable wear excepted. Under no circumstances shall a dirty or broken condition of the premises, appliances or fixtures be considered to have resulted from reasonable wear.

4. **EXAMINATION OF PREMISES.** Resident has examined the premises and has accepted same as habitable and satisfactory. Resident shall have 72 hours after entering the premises in which to examine same for defects or damages and report said findings to the Owner or Owner's Agent. Resident while residing in said premises shall observe and act in accordance with all Rules and Regulations attached hereto and made a part hereof as if fully rewritten herein.

5. **RESIDENT'S RESPONSIBILITY. The Resident Shall:**

   1) KEEP THAT PART OF THE PREMISES THAT HE OCCUPIES AND USES SAFE AND SANITARY;

   2) DISPOSE OF ALL RUBBISH, GARBAGE, AND OTHER WASTE IN A CLEAN, SAFE, AND SANITARY MANNER;

   3) KEEP ALL PLUMBING FIXTURES IN THE DWELLING UNIT OR USED BY RESIDENT AS CLEAN AS THEIR CONDITION PERMITS;

   4) USE AND OPERATE ALL ELECTRICAL AND PLUMBING FIXTURES PROPERLY;

   5) COMPLY WITH THE REQUIREMENTS IMPOSED ON RESIDENTS BY ALL APPLICABLE STATE AND LOCAL HOUSING, HEALTH, AND SAFETY CODES;

   6) PERSONALLY REFRAIN, AND FORBID ANY OTHER PERSON WHO IS ON THE PREMISES WITH HIS PERMISSION, FROM INTENTIONALLY OR NEGLIGENTLY DESTROYING, DEFACING, DAMAGING, OR REMOVING ANY FIXTURE, APPLIANCE OR OTHER PART OF THE PREMISES;

   7) MAINTAIN IN GOOD WORKING ORDER AND CONDITION ANY RANGE, REFRIGERATOR, WASHER, DRYER, DISHWASHER, OR OTHER APPLIANCES SUPPLIED BY THE OWNER AND REQUIRED TO BE MAINTAINED BY THE RESIDENT UNDER THE TERMS AND CONDITIONS OF THIS RENTAL AGREEMENT;

   8) CONDUCT HIMSELF AND REQUIRE OTHER PERSONS ON THE PREMISES WITH HIS CONSENT TO CONDUCT THEMSELVES IN A MANNER THAT WILL NOT DISTURB HIS NEIGHBORS' PEACEFUL ENJOYMENT OF THE PREMISES.

   9) THE RESIDENT SHALL NOT UNREASONABLY WITHHOLD CONSENT FOR THE OWNER TO ENTER ON THE PREMISES IN ORDER TO INSPECT SAID PREMISES, MAKE ORDINARY, NECESSARY, OR AGREED REPAIRS, DECORATIONS, ALTERATIONS, OR IMPROVEMENTS, DELIVER PARCELS WHICH ARE TOO LARGE FOR THE RESIDENT'S MAIL FACILITIES, SUPPLY NECESSARY OR AGREED SERVICES, OR EXHIBIT THE PREMISES TO PROSPECTIVE OR ACTUAL PURCHASERS, MORTGAGES, OTHER RESIDENTS, WORKMEN OR CONTRACTORS.

6. OWNER'S RESPONSIBILITY. The Owner Shall:

1) COMPLY WITH THE REQUIREMENTS OF ALL APPLICABLE BUILDING, HOUSING, HEALTH, AND SAFETY CODES WHICH MATERIALLY AFFECT HEALTH AND SAFETY;

2) MAKE ALL REPAIRS AND DO WHATEVER IS REASONABLY NECESSARY TO PUT AND KEEP THE PREMISES IN A FIT AND HABITABLE CONDITION;

3) KEEP ALL COMMON AREAS OF THE PREMISES IN A SAFE AND SANITARY CONDITION;

4) MAINTAIN IN GOOD AND SAFE WORKING ORDER AND CONDITION ALL ELECTRICAL, PLUMBING, SANITARY, HEATING, VENTILATING, AND AIR CONDITIONING FIXTURES AND APPLIANCES, AND ELEVATORS, SUPPLIED OR REQUIRED TO BE SUPPLIED;

5) WHEN HE IS A PARTY TO ANY RENTAL AGREEMENTS THAT COVER FOUR OR MORE DWELLING UNITS IN THE SAME STRUCTURE, PROVIDE AND MAINTAIN APPROPRIATE RECEPTACLES FOR THE REMOVAL OF ASHES, GARBAGE, RUBBISH, AND OTHER WASTE INCIDENTAL TO THE OCCUPANCY OF THE DWELLING UNIT, AND ARRANGE FOR THEIR REMOVAL;

6) SUPPLY RUNNING WATER, REASONABLE AMOUNTS OF HOT WATER AND REASONABLE HEAT AT ALL TIMES, EXCEPT WHERE THE BUILDING THAT INCLUDES THE PREMISES IS NOT REQUIRED BY LAW TO BE EQUIPPED FOR THAT PURPOSE, OR THE PREMISES IS SO CONSTRUCTED THAT HEAT OR HOT WATER IS GENERATED BY AN INSTALLATION WITHIN THE EXCLUSIVE CONTROL OF THE RESIDENT AND SUPPLIED BY A DIRECT PUBLIC UTILITY CONNECTION;

7) NOT ABUSE THE RIGHT OF ACCESS CONFERRED BY DIVISION (B) OF SECTION 5321.05 OF THE REVISED CODE;

8) EXCEPT IN THE CASE OF EMERGENCY OR IF IT IS IMPRACTICABLE TO DO SO, GIVE THE RESIDENT REASONABLE NOTICE OF HIS INTENT TO ENTER AND ENTER ONLY AT REASONABLE TIMES. TWENTY-FOUR HOURS IS PRESUMED TO BE A REASONABLE NOTICE IN THE ABSENCE OF EVIDENCE TO THE CONTRARY.

7. **OWNER'S LIABILITY.** Owner shall not be liable for any damages or losses to person or property caused by anyone not under the direct control and specific order of the Owner, Owner shall not be liable for personal injury or damage or loss of resident's personal property from theft, vandalism, fire, water, rainstorms, smoke, explosions, sonic booms or other causes not within the direct control of the Owner and Resident hereby releases Owner from all liability for such damage. (If protection against loss is desired it is suggested that Resident secure insurance coverage from a reliable company.) Owner shall not be responsible for any damage or injury caused by the failure to keep the premises repaired if the need for said repair was not communicated to the Owner or Owner's Agent by the Resident and was not reasonably within the knowledge of either the Owner or Agent. Owner shall not be liable for damages if Resident is unable to occupy the above premises as of the _____ day of _____, 19____ when Resident's inability is due to circumstances not within the control of the Owner or Agent. If the Owner or Agent is not able to deliver possession to the Resident within thirty (30) days of the date set forth above for the commencement of the term, Resident may cancel and terminate this agreement.

8. **UTILITY CHARGES.** Resident agrees to pay all charges and bills incurred for water and sewer, gas, electricity and telephone, which may be assessed or charged against the Resident or Owner for the premises during the term of this Rental Agreement or any continuation thereof except those charges and bills which the Owner has herein agreed to pay.

9. **ALTERATIONS.** Resident agrees not to make any alteration or paint or cover walls or surfaces of the rental premises with any material whatsoever without the prior written consent of the Owner or Agent.

11. **EMINENT DOMAIN.** If all or any part of the premises is taken by, or sold under threat of, appropriation, this agreement will terminate as of the date of such taking or sale. The entire award or compensation paid for the property taken or acquired, and for damages to resident, if any, will belong entirely to the Owner and no amount will be payable to the Resident.

12. **PETS.** No pets or animals will be permitted without the prior written consent of the Owner or Agent. Any permission so granted may be revoked at any time by the Owner or Agent.

13. **ASSIGNMENT.** Resident may not assign this Rental Agreement or sublet the premises or any part thereof without the prior written consent of the Owner or Agent.

14. **OCCUPANCY.** Resident agrees that the premises will be used for residential purposes only and will be occupied by _____

_____ and _____

family consisting of _____ persons whose names and ages are _____ .

The premises will not be used or allowed to be used for unlawful or immoral purposes, nor for any purposes deemed hazardous by Owner or Agent or Owner's insurance company because of fire or other risk.

15. **PROPERTY DAMAGE.** In case of partial destruction or injury to the premises by fire, the elements or other casualty not the fault of Owner or Resident, the Owner shall repair the same with reasonable dispatch after notice of such destruction or injury. In the event said premises are rendered totally uninhabitable by fire, the elements or casualty not the fault of the Owner or Resident, or in the event the building of which the above premises are a part (though the premises covered hereunder may not be affected) be so injured or destroyed that the Owner shall decide within a reasonable time not to rebuild, the term of this agreement shall cease and rent shall be due only through the date of such injury or damage.

BREACH OF CONTRACT: In the event lessee(s) is in default of any of the terms or obligations of this Rental Agreement (which includes non-payment of rent, or any rules or regulations herein or hereafter adopted by the lessor for its buildings, its balconies, its courts, its drives, its parking areas or grounds) and lessor requests lessee(s) to vacate the premises as a result thereof or because of said default by lessee(s), lessor initiates a forcible entry and detainer action, by delivering a notice to vacate the premises to lessee(s) as prescribed by Ohio Law, or lessor files a complaint in forcible entry and detainer with the court, or lessor is awarded a judgement order for restitution of the premises, the mere act of vacating the premises by lessee(s) as a result of any of the foregoing acts does not terminate the obligation of the lessee(s) to pay rent for the remainder of the rental period for which no rent has been paid. Lessee(s) remains liable to lessor for all rent and any other damages incurred until the end of the lease term or when the premises are re-rented, whichever event occurs first.

THIS LEASE SHALL NOT BE BOUND BY ANY TERM, CONDITION, OR REPRESENTATION ORAL OR WRITTEN, NOT SET FORTH HEREIN.

IN WITNESS WHEREOF, Lessor and Lessee have executed this Lease in duplicate on the day and year first written above.

LESSOR _____ LESSEE _____

BY _____ LESSEE _____
     OWNER-AGENT/PERSON IN CHARGE

OWNER'S NAME _____ GUARANTOR _____

ADDRESS _____

Addendum

To lease dated _____, _____

This addendum: is between _____ (Owner) and
_____ (Optionee) agree and enter into this Option To
Purchase Agreement.

For And In Consideration: of the sum of _____ ($_____)
paid by the Lease-Optionee to the Landowners, the receipt whereof is hereby acknowledged, the
Landowners hereby sell and grant unto said Optionee the right and option to purchase the following
described real estate, in which the Landowners hold title as an estate in fee simple absolute, together with
inchoate right of dower, for the total purchase price of _____
($_____).

Further, upon the consideration and grants above set forth, the parties agree:

1. **Extent of Option:** This right and option shall extend to, and be effective until _____
   _____ at 9:00 PM.

2. **Exercise of Option:** Optionee to send a certified letter to owner stating intent to finance, to be sent
   anytime within 3 years of this agreement. Tenant must make application and receive either a loan or a
   formal rejection letter. If the latter, owner will grant Optionee a Land Sales Contract, after a successful
   three year tenancy, upon the receipt of the balance of down payment of _____
   ($_____)

The option can only be exercised after receiving their own financing anytime during lease period, or a successful tenancy of prompt rental payments for 3 years. A rent payment is late after the second of the month. Mailed payments must be postmarked by the second of the month. One late payment constitutes a default and voids the option. Tenant can also be evicted based on the late rent, as of the second of the month.

3. **Failure to Exercise Option:** Upon the failure of the Optionee to exercise said right and option in the manner described in this Agreement, said sum of _____

($ _____), i.e., consideration and monthly option payments, shall be the sole property of the Landowners, without further obligation on his part under this Agreement.

4. **Terms of Purchase:** Anytime within _____ years, the Optionee can exercise his right to obtain other funding anytime for a purchase price of _____

($ _____). After the _____ years, and a bona fide institution refection letter, seller will Land Sales Contract for balance @ _____ % interest for _____ years with a monthly payment of ($ _____).

There is no deposit. Rather there is an option fee to be utilized as a down payment only, after a successful three year tenancy at said address, of _____

($ _____). Upon excise of option, an additional sum of _____

($ _____) will be required.

Monthly credits of $ _____ will accrue with each payment of rent. They are to be also to be utilized towards the purchase price in the form of a down payment. These payments will never be refunded, only credited towards the down payment. Their purpose will be only to increase the down payment.

5. **Repairs:** All repairs are totally to be made by Tenant/Optionee. Any necessary repair neglected, i.e., leaks, painting, and broken windows that would cause detriment to the structure or curb appeal, would be cause for eviction and subsequent termination of Option. Tenant/Optionee will have 30 days notice in writing to correct repairs.

Code violation letters must be satisfied by Optionee within the code letter time frame. Otherwise, repairs to be made by Owner and billed to Optionee. The bill must be paid within 30 days or said Option and Tenancy can be terminated by eviction.

Mowing the lawn will be Tenant obligation.

The Tenant/Optionee will not change any colors until a transfer of ownership has transpired.

6. **Existing Encumbrances:** There will be no clouds on title at closing. If they appear, Optionee to give Landowner 15 days extension to clear them. (This does not include a land sales contract where assumable loans remain below contract note.)

Exceptions:_____

_____

7. **Closing:** Optionee to send a certified letter to owner stating intent to finance, to be sent anytime within 3 years of this agreement. Tenant must make application and receive either a loan or a formal rejection letter. If the latter, owner will grant Optionee a Land Sales Contract, after a successful 3 year tenancy, upon the receipt of the balance of down payment of _____

($_____).

8. **Alienability of Rights:** This Agreement shall be binding upon the next of kin, devisees, executors, administrators, guardians, other personal representatives, successors, and assigns of the parties hereto. The rights and options created under this Agreement may be assigned, devised, bequeathed, or inherited by other parties.

9. **Modification**: By mutual agreement of Landowner and Optionee, this agreement may be modified or extended. However, any modification of any portion of this agreement must be made in writing and signed by all parties.

10. **Gender:** All words in this agreement, including the words Landowners and Optionee, shall be construed to include the plural as well and the singular number, words used herein in the present tense shall include the future as well as the present, and words used in the masculine gender shall include the feminine and neuter.

Executed and acknowledged
in the presence of:

_____   _____
                                 Landowner

_____   _____
                                 Landowner

                                 _____
                                 Optionee

CHAPTER 9

INSTALLMENT SALES INCOME

Tax Ramifications For Installment Sales.

Surprisingly, all monies you collect on notes are not necessarily taxable. The government makes allowances for your investment capital and purchase price. Taxes are based on a percentage basis depending on its tax base and profit. The interest portion of the installment payments is always fully taxable and entered on Schedule B.

In the year of sale only, though, you follow the instructions on Form 6252 and make this calculation on the gross profit percentage. Thereafter, just enter the percentage amount and the principle portions of the payments on Form 6252, by which the gross profit percentage is multiplied to find the taxable amount.

Example 5B represents a prime example whereby, on my payment, most of the payment went to the principle, instead of the interest. While landlording, I am taxed on that amount. After selling, I take my tax base and subtract the property depreciation taken over the years, thereby decreasing the tax base. However, the depreciation itself was based upon 27.5 years and really didn't reduce it by that much. The loan term was only 9 years, thereby building the equity up much faster than the snails pace depreciation. In addition, I did increase the tax base a little by adding in the undepreciated balances from the 5 and 7 year expenses.

During ownership, the taxes were paid on that equity build-up even though the money was not actually spendable at that time. In other words, each month a smaller portion of the payment was interest and only that part was deductible, leaving the equity portion taxable.

The good news is that now that the property has been sold, those principle portions of the payment will not taxable again, except for those portions which have been depreciated. The bulk of the principle of my note that will be received, in this example, will be taxed at only 33%.

The bad news is that many lending institutions do not understand the installment sale concept and could refute the larger amount being income and only consider the taxable amount as income. Even though the amount I actually receive is on Form 6252, it seems that they focus only on the taxable amount. Loan officers, I fear, only look at the 1st and 2nd pages of the tax return and then add in depreciation.

Tax Benefits.

Income averaging was a dynamic tool that I utilized years ago. After having a banner year, I could reduce my income by averaging income over a multi-year period. This would blend the annual incomes, making them equal. This would greatly help those who had just graduated from college with new positions and, more importantly, for real estate investors like myself. Unfortunately, that option has been removed by the IRS. So began a quest to replace it with another viable alternative.

Surprise, it is the installment sale method. Why cash out of properties to acquire coffers that only remain until tax time? It would be much smarter to either enter into a 1031 Tax Free Exchange, discussed in Chapter 13, or create Installment Sale Income.

Indeed you are taxed on what you received that year, but possibly at a significant reduction, a percentage, of what you do collect. Based upon Example 5B, a cash out would mean that the entire $47,568.53 would be scrutinized for that particular year. The gross profit would have been $27,354.62. This amount would also have been added to my taxable income for that year. Estimating the tax total for federal, state, and local at 40%, the additional tax burden would have been $10,941.85, leaving only $36,626.68.

Based upon $635.71, an annual income would only be $7,628.52. First of all, the lower dollar amount of $7,628.52 reduces the probability of ejecting you into the next tax bracket because it is a much smaller amount than $27,354.62. Based upon 40%, taxes would only be $3,051.41.

Secondly, you have the advantage of separating out the interest from the principle. Only being taxed on 33% of the principle payments will become more dramatic in savings as the principle increases. In other words, when less of the income is on Schedule B and more on Form 6252, your taxable income will significantly decrease.

Furthermore, the timing is also perfect because as you accumulate more income from additional notes, you may not necessarily pay more taxes based on more income. Rather, the taxable income from the older notes will drop dramatically since a greater contribution would be applied to the principle. Based upon paying just a percentage, thereby offsetting the additional income, you could forseeably enjoy a much higher income without much additional tax liability.

It is possible, however, to have 100% of the installment payments as taxable income. If that is the case, you still have succeeded by spacing out the income.

If you follow my philosophy on investing, you will find that the income from a $10,000 note, $100,000 in notes, or even $1,000,000 in notes is better and, more practical in our society, than money in the bank. Income from notes is power. Income from notes is freedom. Income from notes is financial independence.

CHAPTER 10

NOTES: MAKING THEM WORK

The Big Picture.

Not all of the notes that I have created are impressive and large in face value. Indubitably, by now you have surmised that this is not neither what I, nor my book, is about. When I can profit by $6,547.32 as in Example 6B, I am quite satisfied. Moreover, when I unload a cash flow lemon earning a 2% annual rate of return, and one year even -15% as in Example 5B, and can transform it into a note generating $152,570.40, I am elated.

Collectively, my face value notes range from $4,000 to $76,000. Nearly all of the notes, independently of the others, are minuscule and insignificant to my entire income and net worth. However, when you look at the big picture, which includes monthly cash flow from my portfolio, income from creating mortgage notes, and periodic cash sums from balloon payments, the final analysis is staggering. This, too, should be your strategy, your outlook, and your perception of success. It shouldn't be a couple of sizable notes that can make your house payment, but dozens of small notes that ultimately add up to an executive income and net worth.

Unlikely Candidates.

Nearly all of my examples utilized were not what readers may have expected. Only the fundamentals were textbook type examples. Upon initial observations, they appeared to be small winners at best. Furthermore, in Chapter 5, where I initially lost $209.04 per month after selling, I'm sure you found this quite shocking at first. These selective examples were chosen to illustrate and demonstrate that you can make money where most would think impossible. Fully calculate and analyze all opportunities and then make your decision whether or not to invest in that particular project. As you recall, however, there is more leeway for attempting a project with the Option To Purchase than the other four plans.

A Brief Reflection.

In Chapter 1, I detailed the essence of good qualified buyers. All of these notes that I have worked so hard to accumulate mean absolutely nothing without them. Simply, I felt it necessary for you to read, learn, and understand the installment process so that you could fully appreciate the effort and hard work that it took to accomplish such a goal. I remind you, now, that it is all wasted if you do not follow this one good piece of advice of finding good buyers by running credit checks. Consider it preventative maintenance.

Insofar as Plan V is concerned, owner occupants in single homes are treated differently. In fact, a 3 year trial period is proof

156

of that. Those who survive the 3 years of the rigid payment and repair program will surely provide quality notes as well.

Foreclosing On Mortgage Notes In Default.

Luckily, I have had to deal with only two buyers who did not meet their obligations, one long ago on 5 doubles and the other in 1993 on one double. The default in 1993 was resolved quite easily. My buyer was quite cooperative regarding his default on his $10,500 balloon. He simply brought the note current at closing, paid the closing costs, and assigned the property back to me.

Coincidentally, since the time I had sold that property I had bought the double next door and had begun consolidating in that area as well. In actuality, I wanted the property back in my portfolio. It worked out quite well for me. On the other hand, he did not fair so well. He lost his $3,135.98 down payment and all equity participation over the last 3 years. He did, however, maintain a good credit standing because I wanted the building back and did not demand the full balloon payment. I got the building back, and he got the balloon note torn up. We did each other a favor with our civility.

He had offered to shorten the note and increase the monthly payment by $200 per month higher and increase the interest rate as well. Unfortunately for him, I wanted the property back.

However, on the other default on 5 properties, my quality buyer had sold to a

157

deadbeat who was quite obnoxious and was totally uncooperative. He drained all five properties of every cent that he could and lost them in foreclosure. My seller had to make good on my 5 notes and all five 1st mortgages to someone else as well. All five 1st mortgages and my 5 notes were settled by my buyer. He has yet to receive the first dime from his deadbeat buyer, though. This example fully illustrates how important a good buyer is to you, even if your buyer does not realize it.

Providing that you have a simple note of $10,000, whereby a balloon comes due and you do not want the property back, you can renegotiate the terms. Increase the interest rate by 2 percent on the balance due, write a new note, and eliminate or reschedule the balloon payment. Otherwise, you could turn it over to your attorney and let him collect it for you. Remember, your qualified buyer has some net worth and income.

Your Choices With Notes In Default.
1. Renegotiate your balloon, term, additional down payment, and/or interest rate.
2. Foreclose and have your attorney try to collect balance.
3. Take the property back and resell.
4. Take the property back and keep.

Overcoming Your Fears.
While on the speaking circuit, investors remark that they have been burned before by selling on the installment sale. I ask if they had

done a credit check on their buyer, and the answer has always been "No."

So many times I hear about investors who had one bad experience, and never again will they finance any more property. Their attitude is that they want to totally get rid of the properties and be done with them.

I'm not stating that no loan will ever go into default, rather that a minuscule amount of notes will. The key is to run credit checks. Even I have had to deal with two individuals who failed to perform on theirs. This is no reason, though, to discount the entire note creating process.

For example, if I have two tenants who do not pay rent, does that mean that I quit landlording? Absolutely not. It simply means that I stay on top of the game by holding full deposits and beginning evictions immediately. I build in provisions to protect myself.

If my car doesn't start and I get stranded somewhere, does that mean that I should never drive again? Does it mean that I never leave town anymore? More realistically, it means to insure that the car is in good repair before even leaving the driveway. More certainly, I would not leave town with the car on the fritz. Adding provisions like these would make driving a car more pleasurable.

Inserting provisions is simply what I am recommending to improve, and make success-ful, the installment sale process for those who haven't developed the right frame of mind yet, **an installment sale mentality**. No offense, but selling with no money down to indigents is idiocy. Surprise, the provisions are to run credit checks, get down payments, and leave a cash flow margin so that your buyer can make his payments.

Why, And When To, Sell On Land Sales Contract?

In Ohio, a good way to sell is by Land Sales Contract with far less than 20% down. If it is going to default, odds are it will before the time his equity position reaches 20% of the purchase price. The reasoning for this is that you can regain the property from a Land Sales Contract by filing an eviction, after a 30-day notice, when the equity position is below that 20% or within 5 years; afterward the deed is transferred. (Check your laws.) Otherwise, if your buyer is sitting on the deed, it could take six months in Ohio to fully foreclose. Consult with an attorney for the legal specifics of your state.

Land Sales Contracts are best utilized when you have a very high equity position, are able to carry large notes, and when you are willing to actively participate after a default, as in Plan V. If you are just carrying small notes and you want to get the deeds out your name, like I often do, transfer the deeds.

Selling Your Notes For Cash.

There are financial institutions, investors, and investment companies who actually pay cash for your mortgage notes from 70% to 86%

of their face value. (Investors will sometimes pay 100% if you guarantee them.) This is one way to cash out if you need money. Personally, I haven't sold any notes yet because I have wanted the full benefit of my labors. I may, however, do so in the future if it is necessary to fund a great deal. I do know investors who have sold theirs, though. If I need cash, however, for a real estate purchase in the future, I know where to turn.

These companies also desire good quality notes and therefore do credit checks on your buyers (keep credit info on file) and sometimes inspect the properties. These investors and companies can be found in the investment and residential section of the Sunday newspaper, at local real estate association meetings, in the telephone directory, and by asking someone who has been an avid real estate investor. For further information, go to Chapter 11, Item 5, The Note Broker Business. It will also list two national newsletters that sometimes advertise buyers.

Lifetime Income Outlook.

After examining the two examples featured in Chapter 5, where I entered into delayed note returns, it would be a great opportunity for me to explain my big picture view. It is a lifetime income mindset where I take the focus off cash and onto income.

Mostly, when I explain income, and everyone else, it is done by a weekly, monthly, and an annual interpretation. Particularly in an employment situation, it is the worldwide perception. It is a matter of what you earn weekly, monthly, and annually.

People will ask, "What do you make per year?"

Real estate investors, as well, have the same perception. In fact, it is a matter of what properties made last month or last year, and what properties will net next year. Furthermore, it is also a matter of what the real estate on the whole nets annually.

For example:

"How much rent do you collect per month?"

"What is your monthly cash flow?"

"What does your tax return state that your properties made last year?"

"What do you think the properties will net next year?"

There is nothing wrong with this perception. In fact, it helps to measure how well we, and our properties, are doing in the short term. Regardless of your financial accomplishments, it is important to focus upon figures and situations in the short run to quickly identify deficits, and thereby swiftly making necessary adjustments.

However, I find that after achieving financial independence myself, where monthly expenses are not a concern, there are also times which require a look at the bigger picture, so to speak. Rather than studying my monthly and annual income alone, I find equally as important my **Lifetime Income Outlook**.

This is the outlook which enables me to pursue complex and obscure financial tactics discussed and explained in this volume. It is not such a matter of brilliance or intellect to pursue, formulate, or implement these Plans as it is an ability to glance into the future and perceive your income as lifelong income.

The only time, I believe, that people are subjected, forcibly, on my lifetime income concept is when they buy a home and the financial details of repayment are disclosed. Applicants find that over a 30 year period if they borrow $200,000 at 10% for a home loan they will repay $631,851. It is my contention that this is the closest most will get to my Lifetime Income Concept.

Plan II with delayed note returns where I created two alligators is the essence of what I mean when I discuss this lifetime outlook. Granted, the other four plans play an integral role as well. In fact, when everyone else is chasing the smaller and more immediate buck when flipping for cash, I am going for the larger note with interest, income, and taxes in mind for the long term. When I compare $5,000 in cash now to a $10,000 note with interest for 10 years, I am again considering my lifetime profit picture. That picture shows me that $10,000 @ 10% for 10 years is $15,859.20.

What's the bottom line? The other investors who choose to take $5,000 cash now are losing out.

This perception was probably developed because of my satisfying my own financial needs and my ability to examine my situation objectively. I admit, it is much easier to do when you don't need money.

This is the broad scope of my future. Many notes for many years, of all variations, are the strategy which compliments the lifetime perception of income.

Can you contemplate working a typical job, just starting out, and trying to achieve a net worth of $100,000? I can't. How could you save that much cash? That amount would be insurmountable! Hopefully, in time, you could build up equity in your residence after many, many years.

What if you decided to get off that fast buck mentality and latch onto my note building concept? On 10 of the smaller deals, where you carry $10,000 on each note, you would achieve $100,000 in notes in a realistic amount much time; like while you're still young. This $100,000 in notes is respected and considered as assets, income, and figured into your net worth, even to that obnoxious banking industry.

Imagine what it would be like to have the notes that I do, the income from the notes that I have. It does seem a bit unbelievable. It is bizarre, I concur. Frankly, I can't believe it myself sometimes. It is truly, too good to be true. May I suggest that you get with the program, and soon?

Summary.

For the most part, I believe that nearly all of my detailed information regarding note creation in the five plans was easily understood and learned by my readers. However, Chapter 5 may have given you a little difficulty. If so, after some intense study and analysis you should be able to absorb all the concepts involved with my abstract applications. Perhaps some review with a fellow investor will aid with your comprehension.

Your true testimonial will be when you can take my fundamental and abstract thoughts and actually apply, and even modify, them to your own particular situations with great success. Modifications include interchanging 2nd mortgages, Land Sales Contracts, wraps, personal notes, cognovit notes, and interest rates within the parameters of your state laws. Furthermore, mixing my plans with you own ideas to construct your own strategy, to better adapt to a unique situation, will prove that you have fully consumed my information and are well on your way on that long road to amassing executive income and wealth, i.e., financial independence.

Thus far, investors respond to these note creating methods by exclaiming, "Now I know how the banks make money."

My response to them is, "I don't even need money for my notes!"

My mortgages, in essence, are like they have been created out of thin air, like counterfeit. (Only legal.)

Good Luck. Now go out and print some money,-----some paper money!

PART 2
MORE INVESTMENT
OPPORTUNITIES
AND PERSPECTIVES

CHAPTER 11

THE LATEST TRENDS: INVESTMENT STRATEGIES

Five Rated Strategies.
1. The Seven Year Loop.

When it comes to bank financing, I have been able to avoid it on my inner city properties because of seller financing. Insofar as refinancing is concerned, I leveraged once and have regretted it to this day. Consequently, I'm not fluent on the ins and outs of bank financing. This could be interpreted as my one weakness, or construed as my strongest asset.

During a discussion with a friend of mine in late 1993, he stated that he had just refinanced one million dollars in mortgages. He also stated that this amount is the maximum loan amount at most of the small mortgage companies. He indicated that he had other large loans at other locations as well. I surmised that the low interest rates at the time were the reason for his refinancing. He explained that the current low rate only stepped up the process because he had to refinance soon anyway. (It's been my strategy to pay mortgages off as quickly as I could and stay away from the bank.) Also, I always thought that when investors refinance the only reasons were to leverage and suck properties dry of their equity, or to obtain a lower interest rate.

At this point, we both realized that I had a total lack of understanding of what he had just said. I had absolutely no idea of what he was talking about, and he was shocked that anyone with my knowledge was so inept in bank financing and amortization. Apparently, I was the last real estate professional to learn this refinancing technique, predicament, that he was about to tell me.

He explained that you initially get a 15 year loan on a property, usually a variable interest rate on 5 units and above. On very large mortgages, you are forced to refinance every 7 years. He confessed, "When you have millions in mortgages, the cash flow cannot sustain the tax burden."

Still, I did not comprehend. Logically, the rents have increased much more over the last seven years than the variable payment. Therefore, the owner would still be better off now than the date of purchase. Insofar as taxes are concerned, if you make more money and don't have shelters for that income, just pay the taxes, or buy and finance additional property. I still didn't get it.

He continued by stating that the problem was not overall income, not cash flow, nor leveraging. The fact of the matter, and harsh reality, is that after 7 years the principle portion of the payment increases and the interest part decreases. In other words, you will need to pay taxes on the equity build-up. You don't receive the cash, yet you are taxed on it just the same. Unless you are a trust fund baby, you will be unable to meet your tax liability. Hence, the endless 7 year refinancing, The Seven Year Loop, as I have coined it.

I posed the question, "When does it end?"

He replied, "I don't know. I think never. In fact, I don't think that my properties will ever be paid off."

It reminded me of a phrase that someone else had coined, "Sad, but true."

We concluded that things really were not as bad as it sounded. He does live quite well, and it sure beats working for a living. He did confide that if he were to start all over again, he would invest the way I had and get his properties paid off. (I've heard that so many times it is routine.)

Analysis.

When people divulge their strategies to me, it mostly ends in my feeling sorry for them. There are so many holes in their strategies. Before implementation, investors should weigh the pros and cons associated with them. Jumping in and finding out the hard way is sometimes irreversible, like in this case. My *stay away from banks* starting out strategy would certainly have helped my friend avoid this pitfall.

My advice for investors in this boat is to sell out within the guidelines of your financing just as soon as your equity allows you to do so. Hopefully, it will be before the necessary refinancing takes place. If not, so be it. Just unload as soon as possible and find another strategy, a well thought out and proven plan would be best, kitchen tested, so to speak. Possibly, you could end up with one loan-free project, rather than a multiplicity of losers.

This does not mean, however, that you never obtain bank financing for more expensive complexes in suburbs. It simply means that make sure that either your down payment is large enough to substantiate the tax liability, or you have enough income from elsewhere to cover the equity income. I am convinced that any property with zero percent, or very low, equity is not the solution, but the problem. This problem is magnified on apartment complexes.

THUMB'S DOWN

2. Sandwich Leases.

Some owners do not wish to sell their properties, but will agree to rent long term, over 2 years. You will be allowed to sublet for a higher amount. The owner is guaranteed the rent from you for the lease term, even for ten years or more. Cash flow should be in the $200 plus per month range. You are the middle man, hence the name.

To help convince owners to enter into this lease, you could make yourself responsible for all of the minor repairs. This is an attractive feature for someone fed-up with tenants. You, in turn, also have your tenants responsible for the minor repairs.

Analysis.

One good thing could come of this method, i.e., you could get first dibbs on the purchase of the property. He may not give you the Option To Purchase now, but maybe he will in time.

All else is negative. If the tenant doesn't pay rent, you pay it. If the tenant destroys the house, it's your expense. You are engaging in all the landlord responsibilities without the full benefits. You don't have the deed, so you don't participate in appreciation or depreciation. If you are big into leveraging, you lose that benefit as well. This is bad. Real bad.

From an owner's standpoint, one recently spoke of one sandwich investor who stated that the house was vacant and his buyer wasn't collecting any money, therefore would not pay him. (I would recommend that if you permit another investor to sandwich lease one of your properties, run a serious credit check.

THUMB'S DOWN

3. Lease With The Option To Purchase.

Many investors are also sandwiching Lease-Option contracts. With this method, you make yourself responsible for minor repairs and you then rent on a Lease-Option with your tenant again responsible for all minor repairs. This twist begins to buffer some of the drawbacks. In essence, there will be two Lease-Options written.

This strategy is quite simple. Find a seller in the $30,000-$90,000 range who will Lease With The Option for you to buy on a single house. You Lease-Option, sublet, to a tenant/buyer for $100-250 per month profit.

Ideally, you have a Lease-Option for 5 years. Lease-Option to your buyer for 3 years when selling early, crediting your buyer $125 per month upon performance. Establish a sales price, then tie its final price by making annual adjustments with the Consumer Price Index (CPI). Use the figure based upon fixed goods in your particular region. If your buyer closes in 3 years, odds are you'll do even better.

If your buyer fails to perform, you will have made monthly cash flow, and sometimes benefit from appreciation. If your buyer performs, you have made some cash flow profits, and more importantly, you get a check at closing.

Another twist is to Lease-Option is to make repairs with your own money, and leave vacant until cashed-out. Figure in 12 monthly payments, repairs, and selling costs when calculating projected profit. You really need to buy wholesale to make it work.

In your Lease-Option contract to your buyer:

> You can have a buyer/tenant before you sign,
> You can get more cash down than just a deposit,
> You sell for a much higher price,

You can credit so much per month
towards purchase,
You can pass minor repairs onto tenant,
You can pass all repairs onto tenant,
You can make all repairs and then sell it
outright.

Analysis.

The best scenario is to have a buyer/tenant before you sign your option. (A friend stated that 50% of his deals were pre-sold.) If your tenant does not pay rent, though, you're on the hook for a big mortgage payment. I'd rather own the properties.

My friend stated that years ago this was his primary strategy and he wished he had stuck with it. He hates tenants, and this aids in avoiding them.

Frankly, I don't like soaking money into a property that I don't own, and I abhor deadlines. (They're like balloons.) It is too risky for me. Some investors, however, don't mind sticking their necks out so far.

Furthermore, I also believe that I can make my better deal now, with the immediate purchase. Once the seller begins to consider what he may get in 2-15 years, he could get greedy and take his mind off his current predicament.

When selling with the Lease-Option, you can inflate the market rent by $50. Your lease can be for 1 to 3 years. If the tenant pays on time for that duration, you credit the buyer with all those 50's, and he uses that toward his down payment on his bank loan.

My slant would be to acquire the deed and sell on Land Sales Contract after a successful 3 year tour with a Lease-Option agreement on cheaper properties with arranged down payments, as in Plan V. I don't like the more expensive homes with tiny cash flows.

For more detailed information, see Chapter 8 or in Chapter 13 in the section entitled *Transformation.* This will explain my perspective and further usage of the Lease-Option.

When a Lease-Option is used to buy or sell your own residence, it could facilitate a transaction when otherwise you could not. For example, I sold a fine home in the suburbs with a $10,000 non-refundable deposit and a rental payment just shy of my PITI. On the selling side, this eliminated the pressure of an empty house with a high mortgage payment. On the buyer's side, being transferred here from out of state without the sale of their home made it impossible to qualify for another home. This way, they could live in the house that they wanted to buy, and get $10,000 credited toward the down payment and also a $400 per month credit for each month rent had been paid. This was of no consequence to me because over $500 of my monthly payment was principle. In essence, we both won. In fact, they called within seven months and expressed that they were ready to close because of an employer buy-in on their out of state home.

On the whole, though, I am evaluating these investment ideas based upon money making endeavors, not as personal residences. Thus, the thumb's up/down does not account for personal residences.

Trend: THUMB'S DOWN
Plan V: THUMB'S UP

4. Land Sales Contracting Single Homes.

Find a fixer-upper house in a blue-collar neighborhood and contract at a wholesale price. Pay cash for the house and repairs. Go to the bank and acquire a loan for the retail price of the house. This will be your seed money for your next project, and so on, and so forth.

Lease With The Option To Purchase for one year with the tenant responsible for all the minor repairs, knowing that virtually no one will obtain bank financing. Investors inform me that, based upon their experience, one to five percent will actually get a bank loan after one year. If the tenant has paid on time for one year and cannot get a first mortgage on their own, you will Land Sales Contract to the tenant/buyer. On the average, $250 per month is made on each deal.

Analysis.

When there is no recourse by a financial institution regarding the transfer of owner-ship, I like the idea of Leasing With The Option To Purchase and later Land Sales Contracting when assured of tenant's ability to make payments.

This almost sounds like a good way to make a living, if the banks co-operated. But each investor admits that the bank has a due-on-sale clause on their first mortgages. The loans are not assumable, nor are Land Sales Contracts permitted on these properties either. I know of some investors who have done dozens of these deals over many years and they swear by it. They insist that no loans have ever been called. I can only imagine the nightmare of banks calling the notes on a million dollars in mortgages. No thanks.

Furthermore, I am opposed to refinancing for the retail price, i.e., leveraging. If the loans were assumable and there was a large equity position, taking a second mortgage back or wrapping it would appeal to me.

For example, if I owed $20,000 on a house that I could legitimately Land Sales Contract for $40,000, without the use of leveraging the technique would get Four Stars.

Trend: THUMB'S DOWN
Plans I,II,III,IV,V: THUMB'S UP

5. The Note Broker Business.

One of the latest waves of investing is becoming a **Mortgage Broker**, and brokering other people's notes. Virtually anyone can become one. You can run the business out of your home. All that is needed is a phone and a fax machine. (Check with the licensing bureau for your state to insure that no license is required.)

In essence, you will be the middle man. What is needed are customers who want to sell their notes and someone else to buy them. Finding institutions to sell the notes to is the easy part. Two of the nationwide newsletters are listed below. Each has tid-bits of information regarding the business, advertise learning seminars, conventions, and, most importantly, institutional note buyers. I called requesting complimentary copies. Both sent me one free copy of each and each indicated that complimentary copies were procedure. Just make a toll-free call.

The Paper Source, Inc.
233 Brookneill Dr.,
Winchester, Virginia 22602
1-800-542-2270

NoteWorthy Newsletter
598 Bosworth, Suite #3
P.O. Box 31451
San Francisco, CA. 94131
1-800-487-1864

When you find someone who wants to cash-out of his note, you get the specifics of the note, call one of your connections, and get a quote. Add in a 10-16% fee for yourself and give the **contingent quote** to your client. (On a $100,000 note, your fee could be $10-16,000!) If he accepts your offer, get him under contract with a weasel clause, just in case your buyer, or institution, later rejects the deal. You will not need to use your money to buy the note, just be the intermediary.

The tough part is finding clients. And it is tough. Countless seminars, books, tapes, and newsletters are sold explaining how to seek out note holders. (One of the best kept secrets is that business and commercial notes are the easiest to acquire.)

The notes do not necessarily have to be sold to an institution. A situation may arise where you can buy a note for yourself at a discount and use it as a down payment at full face value on real estate. This would be the wiser move. This way, you further benefit by keeping your buyer's margin. (This would also be a good time to unload some of your other notes at full face value that you have created. You can use your own notes just as down payments, or barter for the full price of properties.)

Analysis.

I love it. If you can't find any clients, you aren't out much. You need a fax machine anyway. You can't lose. If you sell just one deal per year, you could pick up an extra $5,000 or so.

Even better, consider integrating this concept with my note creation ideas in Plans I-V. What if you wanted to cash-out your own notes? If you had a $10,000 note, you could sell it to a broker for $6,000. (The big institutions charge a minimum of $3,000 per deal. The broker could charge $1,000 for himself on the smaller deals.) You could also broker it yourself for $7,000.

The smartest move to make would be to acquire $100,000 in notes and broker them yourself in a package deal. This way, you overcome the negative aspect of the $3,000 minimum charge each of many deals. An institutional buyer could pay up to 86% and maybe more. The $70,000 that you would get from another buyer/broker is now $86,000!

Keep the property notes separated. Premiums are paid for owner occupied singles, and then to single non-owner occupied. Next is 2-4 units, and diminishes after that. Above 5 units take further reductions. In other words, the last thing you want to do is sell 20 small buildings on one note. You want 20 separate notes, which you would sell altogether.

Whether you become a note broker for others, just yourself, or both, I like this idea. It is certainly conservative enough.

THUMB'S UP

Property Flips: What Strategy, And When?

Timing is everything when implementing the Lease With The Option To Purchase & Land Sales Contract vs. cashing-out. Simply, when you purchase a house for $18,000 with nothing down, this is an ideal property to sell on Lease-Option or Land Sales Contract. Of course, it will have assumable financing, so that there is no fear from bank retributions.

If you wanted to keep the house in your portfolio, rather than going for the $10,000 note, you could Lease-Option for $500-1000 down to sell it immediately. Again, the rent would be higher to allow for rent credits. This house could sell for $38,000 using this method. Providing that the buyer performs, you could have stretched the profit by an additional $10,000.

If I paid $18,000 cash for a rental house, I want to cash-out. I would want my $18,000 back at closing. A house in this situation would set empty until a cash investor buys it, or a homeowner gets a loan. My preference is to go for the cash investor who wants to resell on Lease-Option for $38,000. My wholesale price would range from $23-25,000. I would enter into a 1031 Tax Free Exchange, so that I could defer taxes. Details of this type of transaction can be found in Chapter 13.

When dealing in multi-units, it would be best to Land Sales Contract when holding a high equity position, without a substantial down payment. In most of the plans, a $10,000 note is not enough incentive for me to hold the deed. However, a wrap yielding additional profit could heavily influence me to do so.

Summary.

My conservative outlook is overbearing sometimes. In the final analysis, whatever the investor feels comfortable with will be his epitaph. Once I signed a five year balloon on a small deal, and I couldn't sleep well for two months. I sold the property and found inner peace. Admittedly, my comfort level is quite extreme. In the long run, it has attributed to my current success.

However, all the investment ideas in this chapter have shown levels of proven success for many investors, even for my friend who refinances every seven years. He has the ability to borrow and repay for just about any building or personal item he wants. He lives quite well, and most would perceive that accomplishment in itself as successful. From his standpoint today, however, he wishes that he had taken an alternate route where he could have had properties paid for. Had he done things differently he could have worked himself into a situation where he could have relaxed and reaped even more benefits later.

Simply, some are willing to take more risks than others. You need to find your comfort level and work within its parameters. This is how you find true success and peace of mind.

CHAPTER 12

LOW INCOME HOUSING TAX CREDITS

Federal Trade-Off.

In the 80's, the federal government extended the depreciation schedule from 15 years to 19 years. In 1987, the government was at it again and increased the 19 years to 27.5 years, except this time there was a trade off. Those investors who rehab historical buildings or low income housing units would get tax credits. Credits are not a deduction, rather a dollar for dollar credit that you subtract after calculating taxes owed.

The problem is that the application itself is so thick that it is discouraging to even flip through. You can only imagine figuring out how to correctly fill one out. At the very least, you can call your state agency and ask questions, and even attend seminars offered and conducted by the state. At the end of this chapter, you will find a list of all the state housing finance agencies.

Two Housing Tax Credit Avenues.

There are two facets of low income tax credits: those involving application for repairs only, and those for both repairs and building costs. If you just want to buy a tenant occupied building and make updates in furnaces, circuit breaker boxes, roofs, kitchens, or baths, it is plausible. You can work around good tenants. There is a minimum expenditure of $3,000 per unit. Afterwards, simply make application for the repairs only.

The other and more profitable aspect is to find a boarded-up building, or one that will be vacant at closing, and apply for credits for both the repairs and building costs. The agency will frown on applicants who displace tenants, it counters the objective of the program.

In the final analysis, you are providing decent housing to low income producing families and you, upon receipt of credits, are guaranteeing that these units remain such by adhering to income limitations for future tenants for a minimum period of 15 years. When neighborhoods are blue-collar and welfare, this is no drawback. If anything, it is a further incentive to invest in, and upgrade, these areas. Compliance is easy.

A. Improvements Only.

The program has installed a repair bonus for investors who rehab in certain census tracts, i.e., run down neighborhoods. There is no guarantee that this bonus will be awarded, buy at least you have a shot at getting it. Let me illustrate the difference between a non-bonus and bonus situation.

For example, if your repairs were $12,080.32, ordinarily you would request 9% of that for your annual credit, which is $1,087.23, for 10 years. Over 10 years time, this adds up to

$10,872.30. You get back almost every repair dollar invested in the property.

With the bonus, you take the repair figure and multiply it by 130% and get $15,704.42. Then you would use this new figure and multiply it by 9% to get the new, annual, repair tax credit of $1,413.40. Over 10 years, this amounts to $14,134.00, which actually exceeds the repair input of $12,080.32 by $2,053.68.

B. Cost Of Building And Improvements.

It is much easier to rehabilitate with an empty building. Your repairs can be more extensive, and save in plumbing headaches later, for example. In fact, the more money that you spend now can be included in the tax credit application. Once the credits are awarded, that's it. There is no going back and trying to add subsequent repairs to the tax credit, nor will there be any further tax credit applications considered on the subject property for many, many years.

Furthermore, you can increase the award by including the cost of the building and its lot. For rehabbers, the lot and building merge into one figure. You can also include all soft and hard costs associated with its acquisition, like fees and loan expenses.

By using the same example above for repairs, let's see what happens if the building costs are $10,610. Multiply this figure by 4%. Your additional tax credit request for the building and lot is $424.40 per year. For 10 years, it is $4,244.00.

Couple the $4,244.00 for the building costs with the $14,134.00 in repair costs, and you request $18,378 in tax credits over the next 10 years. You have spent a total of $22,690.32 for the entire project. The units are fixed up beyond code. The mechanicals are such that future repairs should be minimal.

The Kicker.

Not only can you get $18,378 in credits, which about doubles your money, but you can still depreciate the building, $10,610 and expense and depreciate all of the repairs, $12,080.32. After all this, you still own the building and can sell it later. Furthermore, you also make a small bundle on the cash flow, and appreciation, where applicable.

(But for now, discount the depreciation and appreciation and focus entirely upon profits. Depreciation is really deferred taxes and appreciation may not even transpire.)

Based upon my experience, you can net $569 per month on a double renting, like this building, for $350 per side. The annual income would be $6,828 and over a ten year period $68,280. Ordinarily, the cash flow and repair write-offs would be the extent of my profit, $80,360.32 for 10 years. Adding in the tax credits of $18,378 increases the 10 year outlook to $98,738.32, without depreciation and appreciation. After 10 years, sell on an installment sale for $40,000. Overall, profits far exceed the original investment by well over

$100,000, over the 10 year period. And, this is on just one small investment property!

Individuals, partnerships, corporations, and non-profit organizations can apply for and receive Low Income Housing Tax Credits.

State Housing Agencies List

Alabama Housing Finance Authority
Executive Director
2000 Interstate Park Drive, Suite 408
Montgomery, Alabama 36109
(205) 244-9200

Alaska Housing Finance Corporation
Executive Director
520 East 34th Street, 2nd Floor
Anchorage, Alaska 99503
(907) 561-1900

Arkansas Development Finance Authority
President
P.O. Box 8023
Little Rock, Arkansas 72203-8023
(501) 682-5900

California Housing Finance Agency
Director
1121 L Street, 7th Floor
Sacramento, California 95814
(916) 322-3991

Colorado Housing and Finance Authority
Executive Director
1981 Blake Street
Denver, Colorado 80202-1272
(303) 297-2432

Connecticut Housing Finance Authority
President
999 West Street
Rocky Hill, Connecticut 06067-4005
(203) 721-9501

Delaware State Housing Authority
Director
18 The Green
Dover, Delaware 19901
(302) 739-4263

District of Columbia Housing Finance Agency
Executive Director
1275 K Street, N.W., Suite 600
Washington, D.C. 20005
(202) 408-0415

Florida Housing Finance Agency
Executive Director
227 North Bronough Street, Suite 5000
Tallahassee, Florida 32301-1329
(904) 488-4197

Georgia Housing and Finance Authority
Executive Director
60 Executive Parkway South, Suite 250
Atlanta, Georgia 30329
(404) 679-4840

Hawaii Housing Finance and Develop. Corp.
Executive Director
677 Queen Street, Suite 300
Honolulu, Hawaii 96813
(808) 587-0640

Idaho Housing Agency
Executive Director
P.O. Box 7899
Boise, Idaho 83707-1899
(208) 331-4882

Illinois Housing Development Authority Dir.
401 North Michigan Avenue, Suite 900
Chicago, Illinois 60611
(312) 836-5200

Indiana Housing Finance Authority
Executive Director
115 West Washington Street
Suite 1350, South Tower
Indianapolis, Indiana 46204
(317) 232-7777

Iowa Finance Authority
Executive Director
100 East Grand Avenue, Suite 250
Des Moines, Iowa 50309
(515) 242-4990

Kansas Department of Commerce & Housing
Division of Housing
Undersecretary for Housing
700 SW Harrison Street, Suite 1300
Topeka, Kansas 66603-3712
(913) 296-2686

Kentucky Housing Corporation
Executive Director
1231 Louisville Road
Frankfort, Kentucky 40601
(502) 564-7630

Louisiana Housing Finance Agency
President
200 Lafayette Street, Suite 300
Baton Rouge, Louisiana 70801
(504) 342-1320

Maine State Housing Authority
Director
P.O. Box 2669
Augusta, Maine 04338-2669
(207) 626-4600

Maryland Community Development Admin.
Executive Director
100 Community Place
Crownsville, Maryland 21032-2023
(410) 514-7500

Massachusetts Housing Finance Agency
Executive Director
50 Milk Street
Boston, Massachusetts 02109
(617) 451-3480

Michigan State Housing Development Auth.
Executive Director
Plaza One Building, Fifth Floor
401 South Washington Square
Lansing, Michigan 48933
(517) 373-8370

Minnesota Housing Finance Agency
Commissioner
400 Sibley Street, Suite 300
St. Paul, Minnesota 55101
(612) 296-7608

Mississippi Home Corporation
Executive Director
207 West Amite Street, #13
Jackson, Mississippi 39201-1205
(601) 354-6062

Missouri Housing Development Commission
Executive Director
3770 Broadway
Kansas City, Missouri 64111
(816) 756-3790

Montana Board of Housing
Administrator
2001 11th Avenue
Helena, Montana 59620
(406) 444-3040

Nebraska Investment Finance Authority
Executive Director
1033 "O" Street, Suite 218
Lincoln, Nebraska 68508
(402) 434-3900

Nevada Housing Division
Administrator
1802 North Carson Street, Suite 154
Carson City, Nevada 89701
(702) 687-4258

New Hampshire Housing Finance Authority
Executive Director
P.O. Box 5087
Manchester, New Hampshire 03108
(603) 472-8623

New Jersey Housing and Mortgage Finance
Agency
Executive Director
3625 Quakerbridge Road, CN. 18550
Trenton, New Jersey 08650-2085
(609) 890-8900

New Mexico Mortgage Finance Authority
Executive Director
P.O. Box 2047
Albuquerque, New Mexico 87103
(505) 843-6880

New York City Housing Development Corp.
President
75 Maiden Lane, 8th Floor
New York, New York 10038
(212) 344-8080

New York State Division of Housing and State
Renewal
38-40 State Street
Albany, New York 12207
(518) 486-3370

New York State Housing Finance Agency
President
641 Lexington Avenue
New York, New York 10022
(212) 688-4000

North Carolina Housing Finance Agency
Executive Director
P.O. Box 28066
Raleigh, North Carolina 27611
(919) 781-6115

North Dakota Housing Finance Agency
Executive Director
P.O. Box 1535
Bismarck, North Dakota 58502
(701) 328-3434

Oklahoma Housing Finance Agency
Executive Director
1140 Northwest 63rd, Suite 200
Oklahoma City, Oklahoma 73116
(405) 848-1144

Ohio Housing Finance Agency
Executive Director
77 South High Street, 26th Floor
Columbus, Ohio 43215
(614) 466-7970

Oregon Housing and Community Services Dept.
Director
1600 State Street
Salem, Oregon 97310-0302
(503) 986-2000

Pennsylvania Housing Finance Agency
Executive Director
2101 North Front Street, Building #2
Harrisburg, Pennsylvania 17110
(717) 780-3800

Puerto Rico Housing Finance Corporation
Executive Director
Call Box 71361
San Juan, Puerto Rico 00936-1361
(809) 765-7577

Rhode Island Housing and Mortgage Finance
Corporation
Executive Director
60 Eddy Street, 2nd Floor
Providence, Rhode Island 02903
(401) 751-5566

South Carolina State Housing Finance and
Development Authority
1710 Gervais Street, Suite 300
Columbia, South Carolina 29201
(803) 734-3381

South Dakota Housing Development Authority
Executive Director
P.O. Box 1237
Pierre, South Dakota 57501-1237
(605) 773-3181

Tennessee Housing Development Agency
Executive Director
404 James Robertson Parkway, Suite 1114
Nashville, Tennessee 37243-0900
(615) 741-2400

Texas Department of Housing and Community
Affairs
Executive Director
811 Barton Springs Road, Suite 300
Austin, Texas 78704
(512) 475-3800

Utah Housing Finance Agency
Executive Director
554 South 300 East
Salt Lake City, Utah 84111
(801) 521-6950

Vermont Housing Finance Agency
Executive Director
P.O. Box 408
Burlington, Vermont 05402-0408
(802) 864-5743

Virgin Islands Housing Finance Authority
Executive Director
P.O. Box 8760
210-3A Altona, 1st Floor
St. Thomas, Virgin Islands 00803
(809) 774-4481

Virginia Housing Development Authority
Executive Director
601 South Belvidere Street
Richmond, Virginia 23220-6504
(804) 782-1986

Washington State Housing Finance Commission
Executive Director
1000 Second Avenue, Suite 2700
Seattle, Washington 98104-1046
(206) 464-7139

West Virginia Housing Development Fund
Executive Director
814 Virginia Street, East
Charleston, West Virginia 25301
(304) 345-6475

Wisconsin Housing and Economic Development
Authority
Executive Director
One South Pinckney Street, Suite 500
Madison, Wisconsin 53701
(608) 266-7884

Wyoming Community Development Authority
Executive Director
123 South Durbin Street
Casper, Wyoming 82602
(307) 265-0603

NATIONAL HOME BASE

National Council of State Housing Agencies
John McEvoy, Executive Director
444 North Capitol Street, N.W., Suite 438
Washington, D.C. 20001
(202) 624-7710

CHAPTER 13

RESTRUCTURING YOUR PORTFOLIO

When And Why?

Once your portfolio has been established, you have the option to reorganize for profit maximization. It is not always advisable, though, to do so if the timing isn't right or if it conflicts with your strategy.

For example, for many years I have structured my mortgages so that they had short term payoffs, such as eight years. Obviously, my cash flow was temporarily hindered as compared to 15-30 year payouts. From my standpoint, the last thing that I wanted to do was finance or refinance for longer terms simply to increase cash flow. This conflicted with my strategy. What was necessary in my early years of development was to focus on maintaining my status quo and get properties paid down and paid off.

However, there was a time during my earlier years when the federal government changed the tax law eliminating personal interest deductions on credit cards and such. An accountant and I deduced that by selling one loan-free property for $32,000 I could pay off all non-qualifying credit cards and installment loans. Afterward, I didn't have the income from that rental, but I didn't have those interest costs and payments anymore either. In this case, personal expenses collided with my investments.

I cashed-out on that property and I was financially ahead immediately after that transaction.

That wasn't major restructuring, rather a minor adjustment. Sometimes, making only a few changes can improve the operation of your real estate machine. On the other hand, if I had refinanced many properties for longer terms, I would have had more immediate income. That would have been major restructuring. Most investors would perceive that move as smart. But I preferred to pay my dues then, and benefit even more greatly in later years. That was exactly how it had turned out.

One time for major restructuring is after the culmination of many properties being paid down and paid off. After a large net worth has been established, herein lies a great opportunity to virtually get out of real estate, yet keep your income, and finally begin that long awaited business venture. In fact, sometimes you make more income after the sale of buildings. Also, you could decide to upgrade your holdings at this time. For others, they may choose to remain in the trenches and just improve their situations.

Another time for major change would be when you are stuck with properties that you acquired with the wrong strategy. An overhaul may be necessary. It may be advisable to bail out of bad investments as their break-even times occur, replacing them with better and more profitable investments. Study Plans I-V for ways to speed up the break-even mark and hasten the sale.

Making More After The Sale.

The longer you own a property, the easier it is to acknowledge that certain properties will never produce as well as others, for whatever the reasons. These units reduce your overall average in productivity and need to be sold. I prefer to owner finance these at higher prices with lower down payments to credible buyers.

With a 30 year installment method, I unloaded a project where my income during ownership was $4,667 annually and afterward was $4,284. My taxable income on the principle portion afterward was only 42%, based upon the installment sale taxable ratio on principle payments. As the principle part increases, it will surpass the cash flow during my ownership because of the 42% taxable ratio. In fact, had I financed to my buyer for a shorter term, the monthly payments to me would have been higher and even exceeded the landlording income immediately.

If you own a property now and feel that it will never perform as it should, project a realistic sales price, down payment, and amortization schedule of payments. Compare this to your current net, considering tax ramifications, and make adjustments where necessary. Here is a great opportunity to unload a loser, relinquish responsibilities, and retain the monthly income.

Totally Selling Out.

I recommend cashing-out only enough properties to pay off all personal bills, except your residence (it is a great tax deduction), and having $20-50,000 in savings. Installment sales for the balance of your portfolio would keep the income flowing, and more importantly, defer and keep the income level for tax purposes. The last thing you would want to due is to sell everything for cash, even if its in excess of 1 million in cash and you feel that you can afford it. The tax ramifications would be horrendous.

The smarter choice would be to cash-out some for necessary funds, to trade (1031 Tax Free Exchange) into real estate that is very low impact, to hire a highly reputable management company (or son), and to sell others on installment sales.

Selling Off Everything For Notes.

When you decide to go this route, it can be a good one. If you plan on doing a lot of traveling, find a mortgage servicing agency to service your notes. They will provide bookkeeping and collection. (This is also good when you create notes and don't want the added record keeping associated with collection of tons in notes.)

1031 Tax Free Exchange.

The tax laws require you to specify in your selling contract that your buyer agrees to participate in the 1031 Exchange. At the closing, give a **statement** regarding the exchange. You need not perform the trade, having all parties there, at the same time. You don't even need to trade with the party you are selling to. For the most part, that would be a little unrealistic. The two important things to remember at the closing are to state that it is an exchange, and don't leave with any money. All funds are to be left there in escrow.

Within 45 days, state in writing to the closing agent identifying by address the property to which you are trading into. And within 180 days of closing, you must close on said property.

This is a spectacular way to upgrade your holdings. You can sell one smaller building, that you originally bought for $20,000, for $40,000. This $40,000 can be used as a down payment on a much larger property. Taxes will be deferred on the $20,000 capital gain because of the exchange. In fact, you can take two buildings and trade both, the $80,000, into something else that you want to buy. Furthermore, if your timing is right, you could swing a deal where you unload many smaller properties and obtain a large apartment complex. It wouldn't really make any sense to sell outright, pay all those taxes, and then buy a complex.

Upgrading Holdings.

Most investors start out in small apartment buildings, they are cheaper and more prevalent. Those successful enough, such as myself, have the option to remain in this arena or enter the world of apartment complexes.

Everyone I know perceives small buildings as a stepping stone into bigger projects. Conversely, I feel that it can be a means to itself, and remaining in that arena does not constitute an investor in transience. There may even come a time when I make the transition myself, but not because I was on my way to bigger things. Rather, it would be because of the high impact and intensity associated with it and I wanted more free time for lectures.

As my wealth increases, I begin to find that keeping my current holdings, continue to create notes, and only adding low intense properties that earn less income, may be the alternative to my current strategy. It would enable me to accumulate countless more properties without the added responsibilities.

If this is now your game plan, I do not suggest trading everything into a 48 unit complex right away and owing a huge balance. The better alternative would be to find what looks like an apartment complex, whereas in actuality, it may not be. The units will probably not be condo's and will be owned by numerous investors. (If they are condo's, insure that the fees are low or the association is inactive. In time, you could control the association by numbers in ownership.) Originally, it could have been a complex, but the owner sold off one or more buildings at a time. This is an ideal situation for you, so that you can get your feet wet on one building. If it works out, trade into as many buildings as you can in that same complex. If it doesn't pan out to your expectations, you've only bought one 4 to 8 unit building. Keep that one building, or sell it. This would be the more conservative approach. You would not be jeopardizing your hard work you performed over the past many years.

Magnifying Income Now.

When investors discuss improving their situation, it usually involves refinancing one or more properties, of which I am adamantly opposed. If you want money to restructure, simply cash-out one or more properties. Although I profess paying one's dues, there is a limit to that concept. It does not mean keep all the properties for their entire loan term, indefinitely. It does mean that indirectly, but only until you have accumulated many properties loan-free and have reached a high degree of success. Afterward, you can cash-out, or owner finance, properties to soften the burden of landlording or allow more income for personal pleasure.

An opportune direction for such restructuring would be to facilitate final payoffs of properties with low balances. With the cashing-out of one building, you could eliminate many monthly mortgage obligations that will offset, fourfold, the monthly cash flow.

Likewise, cashing-out a property to eliminate personal monthly expenses can also significantly increase your discretionary income. I once calculated that less that $20,000 would eliminate over $1700 of monthly obligations. When invested, that amount of money would rarely net an amount so high. In fact, if I were to cash-out of a property for $40,000, the net effect would even be more staggering. The property in question would never net that amount.

If this is your situation, I would ordinarily propose to continue collecting rent and finish paying out your personal bills. However, if you want to lessen the load now and free yourself up for other interests, sell one building now, so that you don't feel shackled to the real estate. You can benefit now. At some point in time, comfort begins to play an important role in your success picture.

Another way to increase income now would be to pay off a note early on a property that you sold, but are still paying on. Examples 5A and 5B would surely fit the bill.

As of 5-95, in respect to Example 5A, the loan balance was $8,784.93. Paying that note off would increase my monthly income by $318.01.

As of 5-95, in respect to Example 5B, the loan balance was $14,061.51. The monthly income increase that I would immediately realize would be $844.75.

In a retirement, or bill reduction, situation either of these would significantly increase your discretionary income now. If you are not into an acquisition phase, it may be wiser to just pay off two notes like these, rather than put $23,000 into new acquisitions.

Selling To Pay Off Cars.

If you are retiring from real estate (you can still be quite young), take my advice from above and pay off all personal bills, except your residence, including expensive automobiles.

When remaining in the business and cashing-out a $40,000 property, you can eliminate an aggregate of personal bills. First choose the lowest balances with the highest payments. Ideally, to make a dramatic impact, balances would be under $5,000 on each. The balance on your automobiles, or truck, should also be in their final months. For example, I still owe about $3,000 on my truck with a payment of $305 per month. Eliminating bills like this would factor in perfectly with some serious effect on current discretionary capital.

However, selling a $40,000 property with income averaging $569 per month to pay off an expensive car is a whole different story. Permit me to explain by backing into it.

My wife wanted a convertible that stickered at $40,000. I told her that was fine, but I was going to invest the $40,000. Then I would go out and finance the car. She asked, "Why don't you just pay cash for the car?" And I suppose you would like to know as well.

I was driving down the street in my investment neighborhood and I saw a For-Rent sign in a window. As I usually do, I wrote down the phone number, called, and asked if he would like to sell his double. His reply was, "Of course I do, but I have a problem. I have two of them."

That was no problem. I negotiated the deal down and bought the pair for $40,000 cash. The rents were $375 per unit, but I lowered three of them to $350. I estimated that each building would net $569 per month, totaling $1138. Now I ask you, which would you rather have: a car paid for, or $1138 per month indefinitely with a term car payment of $656? With my way, in a few years, I will have a car paid off and the continual rental income. This is the decision I made for myself and this is what I advise for you as well, providing you remain in the business.

Lets answer to the original question of whether or not you should sell a property just to buy an expensive sports, or luxury, car. Absolutely not.

Transformation.

In June of '94, I bought a five unit of brick-row townhouses with a two bedroom house on the rear of the lot, which faced a side street. The house really did not even appear to be on the same lot. In fact, there was a yard behind the row and driveway beside the house separating the two buildings. My purchase price was $70,000.

All the units were rented, but the rents were very low. They ranged from $165 to $225. I immediately gave notice of rent increases on the townhouses to $285. I lost 3 tenants in the first 6 months. The new tenants paid $325 per month. The house rent immediately went from $200 to $300.

Now it is time to weigh my options.

A. Cash-Out At A Higher Price.

This is reasonable since the rents have dramatically increased. Furthermore, a nearby 5-unit row has just listed for $129,000 and there is no house in the back yard. Getting $90,000 cash would be very realistic.

B. Land Sales Contract For A Higher Price.

If the buyer defaults, I can take it back, keeping a $15,000 down payment, and resell it again.

C. Parcel It Out.

I could get a survey to separate the house and its driveway from the row and the larger parking lot. This way, I could Lease-Option and later Land Sales Contract the house for $40,000. In essence, I would have $30,000 left in the row. I could keep the row for rental income. Soon, I could have all 5 units rented at $325 per month with over half of my investment back in a note.

There is one water line entering the end unit feeding both the row and the house. The house would need its own water tap and survey.

D. Get A Partner.

If I wanted cash, but I still wanted to retain some landlording benefits, I could sell half of the row for $50,000 cash and still parcel out and retain the house for rental income or sale. With this method, I would prefer to sell the house for $40,000 on Land Sales Contract ($2,000 down payment) after a successful 3 year Lease-Option had been completed.

This would net me $52,000 in cash, $38,000 in a note, and still maintain half ownership in the 5-unit row, $50,000. In total, the profit outlook could be $140,000.

Of these four options, I prefer C. But there is still another alternative that could even surpass even C or D. How could I possibly improve the selling outlook on this deal?

E. Fee Simple Town Homes.

I could have the property surveyed and separate the row units from each other, still separating off the house and its respective driveway. The large parking lot could be a community lot, or each owner could have his own parking space with a community driveway.

The row should also get additional water lines. I do know of units who share in the water consumption off one tap and owners make divisions in the water bill with sub-meters. If this becomes my selling route, I prefer to have water lines installed for all units, not having just one. In other words, I now have one water line for 6 units, so I would need 5 new water lines.

Depending upon local structural regulations, you may need to install a fire wall on a flat roof by removing roofed sections where the units attach, installing the required fire wall, and hot tarring or rubber roofing the implanted areas. For cases where the roof is pitched and there is an attic, it may be necessary to divide the units within the attic area. It would be advisable to contact your local building inspector to determine exactly what, if anything, is required.

I could Lease-Option each of the townhouses for $30,000. Each buyer could put $1,000 down, pay $375 per month, and make their own repairs. After 3 years of paying on time, their respective down payments and $50 per rental months would be credited to the purchase price and Land Sales Contracts would be given.

Any defaults would lose their $1,000 down payments and their $50 per month option fees. During this time also, my landlording duties would be virtually nonexistent. (Remember, buyers make all repairs.)

When someone cashes-out one of my buyers after signing the Land Sales Contract, I cash-out. No one assumes my non-assumable Land Sales Contract without my written permission. This will help assure my getting paid on my note. The last thing that I want is for my buyer to sell to a dead-beat, I've had that happen before. After a credit check, I could allow an assumption without release of liability. This way, I would have two buyers on the hook.

The 2-bedroom house could be sold for $40,000, either by Land Sales Contract and/or Lease-Option. Each of the five townhouses could be sold at $30,000, totaling $150,000. Together, all six units would bring $190,000. I only paid $70,000.

Do you think that $120,000 face value is enough profit? Can you imagine the payout on $190,000 if all loans carried for 30 years? At 10% interest for 30 years it would total $600,264!

CHAPTER 14

ONLY ONE PHILOSOPHY, MINE

Recipe For Success.

When I analyze the social context in which landlords function, I am amazed that we remain solvent. The way civilians, non-landlords, perceive us, the way we perceive each other, and the way we see ourselves is all wrong. I contend that your philosophy is one of three possible reasons for failure; failure meaning never achieving financial independence.

```
        Philosophy  +  Strategy
              = Mindset
```

Any one of the three, philosophy, strategy, or mindset, can breakdown your entire program. All three areas must be superb for you to survive in the real estate business. The correct philosophy coupled with a great strategy equals the mindset for success. Any weakness in the philosophy or strategy will result in failure. The correct mindset, even based upon my own philosophy and strategy, does not insure success. Without the implementation of the right mindset, you would still fail.

For example, my core philosophy is that everyone should pay rent. My strategy is that when rent is not paid on the first, an eviction notice is given on the second. My mindset is in place. All that is required is the execution of procedure.

When I go to the door and the tenant offers $200 instead of the entire $350, I know that I shouldn't take it. I could rationalize about how he'll pay the balance next week and how I want the money. I know what I should do. I have the right philosophy and strategy, yet I take the money. This is a breakdown in the mindset. I have the best philosophy and strategy, yet I refuse to follow my game plan. There is no doubt in my military mind, failure will soon follow.

Is there any surprise why so many fail? Not to me. In fact, rare is the time when I meet someone else successful in real estate. In which area do most investors fail? Only the investors themselves know where their shortcomings lie in their strategies and mindsets. However, I am certain that their philosophies play an integral role in their failure as well.

I'm beginning to wonder if there are more ways to invest in real estate than there are makes and models of cars. Certainly, I offer strategies and opinions on trendy ideas in this book, and I offer a career strategy in *Streetwise*. Hopefully, you can use all, or even some, of my experiences to move forward onto a successful future. There is a possibility that you could choose someone else's strategy, and it could work for you too. And, that's fine. Just find a very good, kitchen tested, strategy. Insure that you question it thoroughly and are satisfied with the answers, then you've mastered one of the three pitfalls. Still, I contend that only one philosophy will work, mine.

Wrong Perceptions.

But first, you must understand what civilians think of landlords, what landlords think of each other, and how landlords perceive themselves, and why they all think it. What comes to mind is that movie about Scrooge. He was a greedy character, and he had lots of money. I've been accused of being greedy, and I have lots of money. He was the type of landlord who took tenants, families, and threw them out in the dead of winter, at Christmas time. I do that too.

Am I upset that everyone thinks about those similarities? No. Only why they draw these comparisons and the conclusions that they draw from them is what troubles me. Granted, these things are true. There is no cause to be mad. The fact is that the events are indeed true.

Someone called to tell me that he had given two of my *Streetwise* books to an attorney's office and one of the ladies had just given him some feedback. I was half listening because I was watching the end of a good movie, and I wanted to finish it.

I knew what he was going to say anyway. It would be something like, "I've always wanted to get a book published. He must be so proud. It is near impossible to get published. How did he do it?"

But, that is not what he said. He confided, "She said you were **the landlord from hell!**"

Not very often am I speechless, but this time I was. We were both very quiet as he waited for me to respond. I immediately regretted even writing the book, and couldn't wait until rewrite time so that I could dress it up. I was insulted, ashamed.

After about 15 seconds (I bounce back quickly.), I said, "Coming from her, that's a compliment." We both had a good laugh and hung up.

Consider how that remark could have affected me. It could have reached the heart of my philosophy, made me change my strategy, and conduct business with the wrong mindset. My choices would have been to either fail or get out of real estate altogether. (Maybe this is why you have failed, or the reason you got out of the business.)

Why did she think that? What exactly did she read for her to come to that conclusion? I don't know, but I was sure that she had, indeed, read my book. Maybe it was where I was explaining how on certain months, tenants don't pay rent. For examples, in August, tenants would rather attend the Ohio State Fair, or on July 4th weekend, tenants prefer big parties. Could it have been that I begin the eviction process on the 2nd of the month? Whatever the reason, or reasons, I will never know, only surmise.

In the summer of '94, my two sons were extras in a karate movie. After three days of listening to all the hype, they convinced me to go with them. They assured me of a bit part because they held the secret to getting picked. The key was to hang near the girl with the walkie-talkie. When they overheard the call for extras, they would stand up in front of her. Also, they instructed me not to shave and how to dress, I needed to look tough.

This time, the three of us camped out close to her. Not one hour later, a voice came over the walkie-talkie. He told her to send over 20 of the oldest, with beards or mustaches, and roughest looking guys that she had available. I was the third one picked! I was so happy, yet insulted. My sons were not chosen for this batch.

It is possible that when people see me during the week, I sometimes look rough, mean. I drive a pick-up truck and I do often get dirty because I maintain a hands-on approach with my rental properties. People who see me under these circumstances could perceive me accordingly, a Scrooge type. This could explain that misunderstanding.

But that lady in the attorney's office had never seen me. Civilians at large who have never met me, or even know of my existence, feel the same way about me. They feel the same way about you and all landlords nationwide. In fact, we landlords perceive each other in the same way. Furthermore, isn't this how we perceive ourselves as well?

Last September, parents bought school clothes for their children. My tenants were no different. Only they attempt to buy them with the leftovers from welfare checks, which is logically impossible.

I went to a tenant's house on the 1st of the month, and she stated that she only had part of the rent. She confessed, "I guess I bought too many school clothes. I only have $200."

I immediately responded, "Take some back. I'll be back tomorrow for the entire $350." The next day I returned. She had returned enough clothing to pay the entire rental amount.

The next day, I went to another tenant's house who was an elderly lady. She had her three of her adult daughters and all of their children living there with her.

She came to the door and explained that one of her other daughters, who lives elsewhere, came into the house and stole the money out of her purse. I immediately wrote her an eviction notice and told her she had three days to come up with the rent or the eviction proceedings would begin. I suggested that the three daughters who lived there should cough up some of their checks to pay the rent. They didn't, and grandma went to a homeless shelter with two of the children, and the rest just scattered.

I am not upset that people see things as they are. What they see and think about landlords, about me, are true. The problem I have is not with what they think to be true, rather what deductions they draw from them. In other words, the events are true, but how civilians perceive landlords, me, and you is all wrong.

Equally as harmful is that landlords perceive each other much in the same way. Most damaging to obtaining success is that this is also how landlords perceive themselves. These perceptions are all wrong. I believe that this is exactly what leads to most landlords' demise.

What Am I?

Am I the landlord from hell? Am I tough, firm, hard nosed? Am I mean like Scrooge because I put families out of their homes at Christmas time? Are all landlords bad simply because they conduct everyday landlording duties? To the public at large, absolutely.

My Defense.

When I filled my gas tank, it cost $35. What would happen if I told the cashier:

> *"My check didn't come."*
> *"My daughter stole my check."*
> *"I'll pay you Friday."*
> *"I'll pay you next month, if I feel like it."*
> *"I had other bills to pay."*
> *"I got my girlfriend out of jail."*

*"My dad died. I used my money to go
out of town."*
"I bought too many school clothes."
"I'll give you half now, and half later."

Can you imagine that the cashier at the
gas station actually had the audacity to demand
his money right away?

Most will agree that food is more
important than shelter, housing. In fact, when I
was an infantry soldier in Vietnam, we often
slept outside. When it rained, I slept in a sitting
position, leaning against a tree with a poncho
over my head. What mattered most to me, back
then, was eating. I remember that once during a
monsoon, I had dropped my sea-ration cookie in
the mud. I picked it up, brushed it off, and ate it
without hesitation. Food is truly the essence of
survival.

Picture yourself going into the grocery
store for a gallon of milk. I have a baby at home.
She needs her milk. What would happen if she
didn't get it? What would happen if I tried
leaving the grocery without paying for it
immediately? Do you think that I might be
detained?

Within the last couple of years, an older
man was shopping in the Columbus, Ohio area
at a large department/grocery store. He was
suspected of walking outside with a pack of
batteries without paying for them. A big brawny

security guard dashed out after him, and grabbing him from about the neck, took him to the ground. Needless to say, the old man's neck was broken and he was crippled for life, over a pack of batteries. Did he steal the batteries? Does it matter? How much do batteries cost? I'll bet under $10. (I agree that the customer's treatment was wrong. I am only demonstrating what one retailer did to protect his property, his precious batteries.)

Why are landlords subjected to such scrutiny whereas other businessmen are not? It's all right for gas stations, grocers, and department stores to demand payment for goods and services the second they are obtained. Why must a landlord allow tenants to consume a $350 per month apartment and make payments with excuses? Furthermore, when a landlord evicts a non-pay, he is perceived as mean, evil, greedy, rich, and Scrooge-like.

Everyone knows that as a speaker, or writer, if you want to please your audience, you don't discuss religion. Since I need to make this point, I will take exception to that rule.

After negotiating for a 6-unit over one and a half years, we finally agreed on a selling price. While I was sitting at his dining room table writing up the contract, he asked if I had a dad or brother who had written a book. I replied that it was I who was the author. He jumped out of his seat and dashed out of the room, returning with my first book. We had agreed that it was uncanny meeting me under such circumstances.

We went on to discuss the rental income status. The rents were unusually low, ranging from $165-225 per month. One tenant, whose rent was $185, had only paid $85 the month earlier.

He stated that no eviction notice was given, because the tenant was a part-time preacher and he didn't have the heart to give him one. I told him he was doing the right thing, getting out of real estate altogether. His wife, overhearing our conversation, eased into the dining room to save her husband from my wrath.

She stood behind him while he was seated, rubbing his shoulders, and said, "My husband is religious too."

I remarked, "What am I, a heathen? I go to church almost every Sunday," I argued.

She remained quiet, quickly signed her name, and swiftly departed the area for fear that I would change my mind and not buy the property.

What really matters here is that he read *Streetwise* and was knowing of my landlording game plan. Furthermore, I even told him that my first act as owner would be to dart over to that unit and post an eviction notice on the front door. Regardless of knowing this, he signed the contract and sold me the property.

Let me respectfully submit to you that if he were a true Christian, according to his own philosophy, he would not have sold me the building. He, being a true religious man, should have kept the building and let the family live for free until he could find a more suitable buyer with the same caretaker qualities. (In reality, it wouldn't have been very hard. There are plenty of nice guys around.) This man is no Christian, by his own standards.

It's bad enough that landlords are considered mean, evil, greedy, rich, and Scrooge-like. Now they're unchristian.

Am I unchristian because I don't provide free housing? Does an oil company provide a gas station from hell because they want paid? Does a chain-grocer own the grocery store from hell? Does anyone perceive department stores as retailers from hell because they have a cash register at the front door? If it isn't tough, firm, and hard-nosed for stores to require, even demand, immediate payment, why are landlords treated and perceived so differently? Am I saying that the whole world is wrong, and I am right? You bet I am.

Permit me to again pose those same questions that I asked earlier. Am I the landlord from hell? No. Am I mean like Scrooge because I put families out of their homes at Christmas time? No. Am I merely conducting business like millions of other businessmen? Yes. I am a businessman. If you cannot pursue real estate from this perspective, you will most definitely fail.

It is very easy to be influenced by your surroundings. Your immediate sphere of influence, family and friends, can ultimately determine your future. How do you react when you receive a phone call critiquing how you conduct business?

If you mentally cannot function as a businessman, do yourself a favor and get out of the business. In fact, your messing it up for the rest of us. You are training tenants to think that they only have to pay rent when they feel like it.

If your strategy is good, yet you are simply earning a living, change your philosophy. Start anew and refreshed. Join me in the arena of success.

I'll See You---At The Top!

RECENT RELEASES
by H. Roger Neal

Streetwise Investing in Rental Housing
A Detailed Strategy for Financial Independence...$15.95

This 240 page paperback provides a career strategy for landlords investing in the inner city. Learn a methodical procedure for doing business. Profit maximize through a business mentality. Read how to net $136,672.80 annually on just 40 units! Discover that investors don't need hundreds of units to reach the big-time. Novice and seasoned investors alike will learn from this conservative, but profitable, approach.

FAST-FLIP™ for Note Creation
16 CASSETTE TAPE SET
and FAST FLIP™ for Note Creation Workbook-1................................$295

This 16 Cassette Tape Set, with 160 page workbook, was originally recorded on DAT (digital audio tape) to provide excellent sound quality. Recording was professionally produced and edited.

You will find 5 conservative plans to buy and flip properties. Fortunately, Neal doesn't compromise making money with his conservative views. These plans still afford you the opportunity to create a financially independent lifestyle and an executive net worth. Listen as Neal changes your investment objectives from building cash now to creating income with a lifelong income perspective.

Neal feels that cash does not really command the power that income does. Go to any lending institution and find how 1/2 million dollars in savings with zero income compare to zero savings and $100,000 net income per year. Your loan officer will predictably inform you that with the former you can spend that money tomorrow and have nothing from which to repay the loan. An income tax return reflecting a high income demonstrates an ability to repay and is security for those institutions. Likewise, Neal contends it is more secure for you as well.

What Neal recommends is to establish income first, thereby achieving financial independence. After your income and net worth has increased to a high level, then begin to add cash to your coffers. In essence, cash is not a means to itself, whereas income is.

Neal addresses FHA, VA, Purchase Money Mortgages, Lease with the Option to Purchase, and Option to Purchase in *FAST-FLIP*™. He also discloses abstract techniques for selling unwanted properties quickly in Fast-Sell. In addition, those with large coffers now will also find an outlet for those funds in Slow-Flip.

Follow the information found in this book with a 160 page workbook which coincides with the audio tapes. The audio tapes go far beyond his written words in *Techniques*. He includes a vast array of information found only in the tape set.

Treat yourself to 32 sides of an energetic delivery of his expanding topics. You will find the cassette tape set very upbeat, entertaining, engrossing, motivating, and educational. Enjoy!

FAST-FLIP™

Newsletter......................$39.00 for 1 year
$69.00 for 2 years

A monthly publication based primarily on H. Roger Neal's own experience and expertise. Don't be confused by the title, it is simply his trademark. In fact, the newsletter will most assuredly encompass flipping properties, landlording, note creation, and brokering of notes.

Admittedly, landlording is hard work and intense sometimes. Neal poses his own philosophy, business, management skills, and strategies that led to his own success. The newsletter also enables him to keep information current to his readers.

SERVICES

Consulting Services...............fees vary

Investors often find themselves either preoccupied with the operation itself of their real estate machines or focusing on other priorities, overlooking changes that could improve income. Here is the opportunity to find out what an expert thinks of your situation and a chance to fine tune your real estate portfolio. If necessary, you and Neal could overhaul your portfolio together.

In the business world, you here words like restructuring, reinventing, reengineering, downsizing, selling off, profit taking, consolidating, retiring, and expanding. Neal proposes using that same business mentality in real estate investing.

Whether you are flipping properties or landlording, or both, you will find what Neal would do in your situation. The service ranges from single problems to one's entire real estate picture. Experience a consult with H. Roger Neal. Call (614) 792-1579.

Speaking Engagements.

H. Roger Neal is available to lecture throughout the country at real estate associations, conventions, etc.
Call 1 (800) 427-1072.

CALL TO ORDER

1 (800) 427-1072

MC/VISA/AMER-EXPRESS/DISCOVER

OR

MAIL CHECK OR MONEY ORDER TO:

MYRIAD PUBLISHING INC., P.O. BOX 1109, DUBLIN, OHIO 43017-1109

Fax Comments and Testimonials to 1 (614) 799-2397

ABOUT THE AUTHOR

Not so long ago, H. Roger Neal found himself in a the typical situation where he was 28, had a dead-end job, a family to support, and the yearning to become somebody. Based upon statistics, you would assume that it would be unlikely for him to become financially independent. As you now know that wasn't the case.

Over time, Neal has gone against the grain to develop and refine his own strategies on and perceptions of real estate to the degree where he has virtually pioneered a new road for investors to follow. In essence, he has reinvented real estate investing by merging great profits with conservative thinking.